# What Your
# Financial Advisor
# Isn't Telling You

# WHAT YOUR FINANCIAL ADVISOR ISN'T TELLING YOU

THE **10 ESSENTIAL TRUTHS**
YOU NEED TO KNOW
ABOUT **YOUR MONEY**

# LIZ DAVIDSON

HOUGHTON MIFFLIN HARCOURT
BOSTON   NEW YORK
2016

For information about permission to reproduce selections from this book,
write to trade.permissions@hmhco.com or to Permissions, Houghton Mifflin Harcourt
Publishing Company, 3 Park Avenue, 19th Floor, New York, New York 10016.

www.hmhco.com

Library of Congress Cataloging-in-Publication Data
Davidson, Liz
What your financial advisor isn't telling you: the 10 essential truths
you need to know about your money / Liz Davidson.
pages cm
ISBN 978-0-544-60230-4 (hardback)
ISBN 978-0-544-63334-6 (ebook)
1. Finance, Personal. I. Title.
HG173.D335 2016
332.024 — dc23
2015015902

Book design by Victoria Hartman

Printed in the United States of America
DOC 10 9 8 7 6 5 4 3 2 1

The chart on page 63 is courtesy of the Investment Company Institute. 2015. *2015 Investment Company Fact Book: A Review of Trends and Activity in the Investment Company Industry.* Washington, DC: Investment Company Institute. Available at www.icifactbook.org. All
other graphs and diagrams throughout the book are courtesy of the author, including the
DebtBlaster chart, which was developed using software licensed from Highsoft AS, Norway.

*For mom.*

*Your courage has been the greatest lesson of my life.*

# Contents

# Author's Note

**Before you read** any further, please know this: I am not a financial advisor. I have zero investments, insurance, or mutual funds to sell you. I couldn't legally sell them to you even if you asked, because I'm not licensed to sell securities. I don't have a pitch, an ulterior motive, or a quota to reach. And that's precisely why I am the author of this book.

As the founder and CEO of Financial Finesse, I run a company that provides people with entirely unbiased financial guidance, no strings attached, and this book is an extension of that practice. While the mission of this book is to shed light on the limitations of the financial advisor industry and to offer education, support, and insider knowledge that you are unlikely to receive in a typical advisor-client relationship, *What Your Financial Advisor Isn't Telling You* is not intended—in tone or in content—to be an exposé of financial planners or the financial services industry as a whole.

Rather, the purpose of this book is to educate you about the vitally important questions you need to ask about your long-range financial future, whether or not you choose to have a financial advisor. Many millions of Americans put their faith and trust in their advisors, and that's fine. But you really owe it to yourself to know the right questions to ask your advisor. After all, if you can't have a truly open dialogue with your advisor about your money, you may never get on the same page. Furthermore, it is important to bear in mind that if you don't ask, your advisor is not always going to volunteer certain information.

As the employer of a team of elite CERTIFIED FINANCIAL PLANNER™ professionals who work exclusively as full-time financial educators, I know what a unique and valuable opportunity it is to work with exceptional financial planners. These professionals have the extensive training and experience to help people in all areas of their financial lives and a deep commitment to helping others become more financially secure.

The problem with financial advisors does not lie with them as people; the problem is that they work in an industry that is typically not incentivized to operate in the consumer's best interest. Back when the CERTIFIED FINANCIAL PLANNER™ professionals at Financial Finesse were employed at large financial institutions, making a living by selling financial products and services, they were generally limited to working with people who could afford to purchase high-priced financial products and services. They entered the profession to help all people, but the current system didn't always make that financially feasible.

In today's financial services industry, those who most need serious financial help are the least likely to get it, and those who can afford it too often receive sales pitches rather than the unbiased guidance they're looking for. As you will learn in the introduction to this book, this is what inspired me to open the doors of Financial Finesse in the first place — the strong belief and personal conviction that everyone is entitled to the benefits of unbiased financial education. By writing this book, my staff and I now have the opportunity on a broader scale to share financial knowledge that will better equip you to be in control of your money.

This book is being released at a time when the financial industry is moving toward more transparency, which is good news. The even better news is that this book is the tool that will help you capitalize on this new transparency.

# Introduction

## DAN AND MARGIE'S STORY

After Dan and Margie sold their mortgage-free home and moved to Florida, they were $500,000 richer in cash. While transferring their account from their branch in New York, the Florida-based bank teller suggested that they meet with the bank's investment brokers, so they did. After discussions and an evaluation, the broker sold them a variable annuity, in which they invested about $350,000. The plan was for the annuity to generate lifetime income payments to pay for their regular monthly expenses in retirement.

What Dan and Margie didn't realize was that the variable annuity was invested primarily in stocks. When the market took a downturn, their annuity income did too. This meant that Dan and Margie would eventually have to start drawing down their retirement nest egg to supplement the dwindled annuity income in order to cover their regular monthly expenses. In an effort to protect their retirement income, they unintentionally put themselves at risk of running out of money with a product that was too aggressive for their needs.

## REGINA AND MARC'S STORY

Regina and Marc waited a long time to have a baby, and when they did they made three important phone calls: the first two went to their respective parents, and the third went to a financial advisor who had advertised on one of Regina's favorite baby websites. They didn't want to waste any time before setting up a college fund for their new bundle of joy.

Marc, a high school teacher at the most respected private school in the community, knew all too well the financial trouble that many families found themselves in when it was time to apply to college. As a teacher, Marc was passionate about the value of education and adamant that his son would not have to make compromises when it came to going to the college or university of his choice. He was determined to do whatever it took to make sure he and his wife saved enough to fully pay for his son's education.

Marc and Regina's financial advisor explained to them the benefits of a 529 plan: the tax savings, the prepaid option offered by some states, and the comfort of knowing that, when the time came, their son would be able to attend college without taking out student loans. The planner estimated that with a 7 percent increase in college costs per year, they would need to save about $240,000 by the time their son was 18 and going off to school. To reach that goal, the advisor recommended that Regina and Marc sock away close to $550 a month. The problem was that the advisor was only planning for what they specifically asked him—how to save for college—and had asked no other questions.

The next month, when Regina went to pay her credit card bill online, she remembered that she had been planning to use that $550 a month to pay down her hefty $10,000 balance, which she had accrued before she met Marc; she had used her credit card to sustain herself when she was unexpectedly laid off from her job. Since that amount was now being allocated to the baby's future, she clicked to pay the minimum monthly payment and her payment was satisfied for the billing cycle.

When Regina and Marc called our financial helpline in 2009, they had nearly $30,000 of credit card debt. Even worse, after a significant loss due to the stock market downturn, they had only a little more than $20,000 in a 529 plan for college. At the same time, Marc was worried about his own job security in the face of the recession.

We worked with Regina and Marc to find a practical solution to pay off their debt and preserve their college savings, but in the process their lives were turned upside down. They had to temporarily stop saving for college in order to free up funds to pay off their credit card debt, which broke their hearts, especially as they watched the stock market rebound. Marc had to pick up extra duties at his school to generate more income, and he also took odd jobs during the summer. Regina, who had wanted to dedicate her time to staying home and raising her son, was forced to ask her mom to care for him while she accepted a job outside her chosen field. Ultimately, Regina and Marc were both able to develop a strong financial foundation and return to their normal lives, but for several years life was much tougher than they ever expected—all because they didn't pay off their debt when they had the chance.

## TAMARA'S STORY

In her early forties, stay-at-home mom Tamara hadn't contributed to a 401(k) or any retirement plan since she left her last job a decade earlier. In fact, she had been meaning to roll over her savings from her old company's plan into some sort of other account, but she really had no idea what.

Tamara had a firefighter friend who was moonlighting as a financial advisor to keep his own family's head above water, and he suggested that she invest in stocks. He loved the market and followed it like his favorite sports team, he told her. Forecasting that the S&P 500 was going to go above 2,000 that year (it was 2007), he said it was a really good time to get in the game. Tamara signed on the dotted line, thinking that it would be fun to have a friend be her financial advisor.

Did she consider how well her new advisor had been doing with his own investments? Had it occurred to her how odd it was that he needed to pick up a second job as an advisor in the first place? Unfortunately, because they were such good friends, it didn't even dawn on her to ask.

Lo and behold, his prediction about the S&P 500 did not come true, and her account balance dipped below its original value. Panicked, Tamara asked her financial advisor if he would take her out of the market; she had learned that she was pretty risk-averse and wanted him to place her money somewhere more stable. He obliged and put the little bit of retirement money Tamara had left into bonds from the safest company he could think of—General Motors.

Fast-forward just a few years: those bonds were practically worthless. Ironically, had Tamara's financial advisor discouraged her from selling when the market dropped in 2008, she would have ended up with a significant gain by 2014. Instead, she lost a substantial portion of her life savings in his well-intentioned effort to keep her money "safe."

## SCOTT'S STORY

Scott, a factory supervisor, was anxious to make some quick money so he could support himself as he made the transition from managing a production facility to driving a race car for a living—his lifelong dream and something he'd been doing as a hobby for more than a decade. He inherited a $200,000 IRA after his great-aunt passed away, and he decided this was the perfect opportunity to build the small fortune he would need to make the transition.

The market had just recovered, and his brother-in-law, who was a broker, convinced him it was time to invest in growth stocks. He was right, and within a couple of years Scott had what he thought was enough to pursue his dream, so he quit his full-time job and dedicated himself to perfecting his racing skills.

By the time we talked with Scott, he'd had to give up his dream and go back to work to help pay the federal and state income taxes on the IRA distributions—something that was never discussed when he started investing. His brother-in-law, who had been a financial professional for 20 years, simply assumed that Scott knew the tax bill was coming and never thought to bring it up.

## NOBODY CARES MORE ABOUT YOUR MONEY THAN *YOU* DO

These stories have a moral to them: nobody cares more about your money than you do. Not the man who sits behind a desk at the bank, not the ex–college buddy with the fancy title "Financial Advisor" on his business card, and not the famous TV personality who professes to know the next "hot" stocks. But none of these people will tell you that.

How do I know? I didn't always know. I once believed, like everyone else, that if you have money, the financial services industry will take the best care of it for you, and that if you don't have money, well, the same industry can help you make some. When I went to business school, I rubbed elbows with a lot of future financial service providers—I even became one myself, graduating and running a hedge fund with a partner. That's when my education *really* began.

It was the dot-com boom—1999—and people were willing to invest in just about anything. At the hedge fund, it was my job to gather capital by meeting with high-worth investors, talking to them about why our fund was superior, speaking at conferences, and generally promoting our fund along with our particular investment strategy. My partner's role was to do the investing.

Hedge fund investors, by and large, are very smart and interesting people. Back when we ran our fund in the late '90s, the Securities and Exchange Comission (SEC) required that hedge funds be sold only to investors who made $250,000 a year or more or had at least $1 million in net worth. Hedge fund investors came from a range of backgrounds, but were generally highly successful and considered to be sophisticated investors by the SEC. Among this elite group were doctors, lawyers, business owners, serial entrepreneurs, and financial people themselves. All of them were clearly intelligent and knowledgeable about a great many things—*as long as those things had nothing to do with their money.*

What do I mean? Most of them simply didn't understand the principles of investing. And many of the finance industry people thought they knew so much that they attempted to beat the market, usually with not much success.

During this era, when people were becoming overnight millionaires by investing in dot-coms being run out of someone's basement or garage, it became challenging to keep our clients in the fund.

We managed to avoid a mass exodus, but I felt like I was seeing a car crash in slow motion. I watched many of our investors begin to get involved in the dot-com boom—investing large amounts of their portfolio in highly risky tech investments without thinking through the consequences. Some of the people we talked to were even getting into day trading. As a value-oriented fund, we were more conservative than most and a bit of a hedge against the other investments these people were making, but I began to question whether I was really operating in the best interest of our investors. They needed financial planning guidance and I was selling them yet another hedge fund option, which didn't fully protect them against their more risky investments. I was a salesperson, with one product to sell, when they really needed someone who could help them navigate what appeared to be an increasingly dangerous stock market bubble.

*These people need to be diversified!* I said to myself. *How can such successful people not know this?*

They didn't seem to understand that they were playing with fire and that our fund, while conservatively invested, was not sufficient to fully hedge their bets when the market collapsed. Moreover, why were these supposedly intelligent people overspending, taking on high-interest debt, and borrowing to exercise stock options that were in no way guaranteed to ever make any money? How could they believe that the dot-com era wasn't a bubble? Why were they not preparing for the fallout?

Then my imagination really began to run wild. If these kinds of basic mistakes are being made by people who have enough money to rebuild their portfolios in the event of a catastrophe and who can afford to hire accountants and brokers and their own financial advisors, then what about the average person? What about people who have little, if any, savings and no access to expert advice? If something happens to them, who helps them get out of the hole and reset? Who helps them not get in a hole in the first place?

I wanted to scream at my clients, whom I realized didn't know any better how to manage their money, "You need a real financial plan! This is not the right way!" But if I did, my partner would have deemed me insane. We would have gone out of business.

So I kept doing my job and did it well, while I found a way to do penance and ease my conscience. I started conducting free workshops with a financial planner so that regular, hardworking people could receive an education about their financial health without being required to buy something in return. In fact, I wasn't getting anything from the workshops, at least not financially. Because the attendees didn't meet the criteria, none of them were allowed by law to invest in my hedge fund, so I couldn't use the workshops as a marketing tool to lead capital to the fund. As a result, I was able to make my workshops completely unbiased and keep them focused on the bigger financial picture—the one beyond just investing.

I didn't know it then, but these workshops were the precursor to my company Financial Finesse, which opened in 1999 as the first unbiased financial education firm of its kind in the country. In short, I quit the hedge fund business and got into the business of helping people manage their personal financial situations holistically. Since its inception, Financial Finesse has partnered with Fortune 500 companies and other businesses, large and small, to provide free, unbiased financial training to their employees as a part of their employee benefits package. We do not work with individuals because we don't want them to pay out of pocket for individual financial planning. By working on the corporate level, Financial Finesse can ensure that employees get the help they need with the cost completely absorbed by their employer. With this book in hand, you now have access to the same lessons, guidance, and wisdom that we offer daily at Financial Finesse through our workshops, one-on-one consultations, and financial helpline.

I wrote this book to be an extension of my passion for education and to shed some light on how the financial services industry is set up to operate. By its very nature, that industry can lead unknowing people into financial binds, as it did for Dan and Margie, Regina and Marc, Tamara, and Scott. What were their financial advisors not telling them? A lot, as you'll discover in this book.

Just as it would not necessarily have been in the best interest of my hedge fund had I deterred clients from choosing to invest their money in the fund, today's financial planners and advisors face the same conundrum. They're not necessarily unethical, unscrupulous, or overly greedy (though, of course, there are always a few rotten apples in every barrel). Because their livelihood depends on what *they* can earn from *your* money, however, there are some things that your financial advisor just isn't telling you.

## HOW TO USE THIS BOOK

Everybody approaches a new book in his or her own way. Some read the back cover first, while others go through the table of contents. Some jump right in and start to read. Others flip to the last chapter and start there.

It's the same regarding personal finances. I am pretty sure that one person's financial picture looks nothing at all like someone else's. Everybody has his or her own style of managing his or her money, and rightly so.

That's why I have written this book in a way that I hope will be accessible and customizable to your personal financial questions, needs, and goals. Each of the 10 chapters is dedicated to one essential truth about finances that your financial advisor isn't telling you. Each chapter then provides what Financial Finesse is known for: anecdotal, research-based, and, most important, *unbiased* guidance in incorporating this essential truth into your own financial life. It is this new financial knowledge and guidance that I hope will change your outlook and help you finish this book with a renewed commitment to take control of your finances.

Building and operating Financial Finesse for going on two decades now, I have witnessed the power of continual support, holistic education, heartfelt encouragement, and goodwill, especially when working with people who have become somewhat cynical and distrustful and are desperate for the truth about their finances. Therefore, the tone of this book is meant to be not only inspirational and informative but also, and most importantly, empowering. Just as we don't blame our doctors if we end up with type 2 diabetes, develop cancer, or have a heart attack, I want to empower you to look at yourself objectively—your habits, behaviors, and lifestyle—as a first step toward financial wellness.

Doctors diagnose our illnesses and treat or manage them, but no doctor can actually *make* us healthy. The same thing is true regarding financial health. No financial advisor can *make* you financially secure. The right advisor certainly can help, but it's your decisions, day in and day out, that ultimately determine your financial health. And most of those decisions have nothing to do with what a financial advisor focuses on—a truth that is the crux of this book.

*What Your Financial Advisor Isn't Telling You* demystifies the actions and advice of many financial advisors while also revealing 10 essential truths about how to build and secure wealth. Here are just a few examples of what you'll find on the following pages:

- Access to the DebtBlaster Strategy—a unique way to cut down your debt faster than you think and save significant money at the same time
- The reasons why the best-performing mutual funds typically make for the worst investments

- The three things to do to maximize your chances of a high return on your investments
- Research proving that your daily financial stress can give you a serious illness
- How to make peace (or at least call a cease-fire) if you and your life partner have become financial enemies
- How to determine and then track on a quarterly basis what you are *really* worth as a way to reduce debt
- Why it's perfectly legal for anyone to set up shop as a financial advisor and where that leaves the rest of us
- How to spot bogus advisors so you don't end up investing with the Bernie Madoffs of the world
- How to select and manage financial advisors to ensure that their first fiduciary responsibility is to you
- How you can help change the structure of the financial services industry so that every American has access to the unbiased financial guidance they need and deserve

The book's appendix is a step-by-step checklist for creating your own Financial Independence Day—an entire day devoted to taking control of your finances so that you can begin your own journey to becoming financially secure and independent, whether or not you choose to use an advisor to help you.

Financial independence can be attained, but like life itself, it is not without its ups and downs, its twists and turns. Nevertheless, though it's not easy by any means, it's also not as complicated as the financial services industry would like you to believe. The secrets lie in the 10 essential truths that the financial services industry and its hundreds of thousands of financial advisors aren't telling you. Learn them here and discover that the best-equipped financial advisor you'll ever meet is the one staring back at you in the mirror.

Happy reading!

*Liz Davidson, spring 2015*

# 1

## Keep Your Money Where You Make Your Money

**The biggest secret** that the financial services industry doesn't want you to know is that your employer is almost always your best financial services provider. Whether you love or hate your job, even the best financial advisor can't compete with the benefits provided by your company. And your employer provides you with the most important benefit of all—your paycheck, which, if you save and invest it appropriately, is like rocket fuel when it comes to driving your own financial security.

Our Think Tank at Financial Finesse estimates that an employee could leave as much as $1 million on the table over the course of his or her career by not taking full advantage of company benefits. Think about that for a minute. One million dollars—how would that change your life? And *why* does no one tell you this? You'd think that, with all their expertise, financial advisors would be all over this route to financial security, the same way the pharmaceutical industry would love to find a cure for the common cold.

And what a huge difference this would make to so many Americans. It would change our economy and the prospects for our children and grandchildren. And yet most financial advisors ignore, or at the very least minimize, your employee benefits. Why? How is it even possible that they would overlook something so big?

The answer comes down to money (as most things do). The vast majority of financial advisors serve the retail market—meaning that they don't get compensated at all when you invest in your company benefits. It's not that they want you to ignore your benefits, but you are coming to them with money to invest or protect, and they are paid based on the investments and insurance they sell or manage for you. There is simply no incentive for them to work with you to maximize your company benefits. At best, they would be spending valuable time and not getting compensated for their efforts. At worst, you might discover that your company benefits provide you with sufficient opportunities to grow your wealth and that you actually don't need an outside advisor.

Just like you, financial advisors have to put food on the table. If a task was not part of your job description, you didn't get anything extra for doing it, and it actually took you away from opportunities to excel at your job, would you do it? Probably not. And as a general rule, neither will most financial advisors.

There's another reason most employees don't think about their employer as their best financial services provider and the easiest means to financial security. I call it the Happy Hour Phenomenon, and I fell into it big-time when I was in my first job just out of college.

Who doesn't love Happy Hour? It's a workplace necessity, a reward at the end of a long workweek, a ritual through which lifelong friendships are sealed. But what an oxymoron! Because anyone who has been to a Happy Hour (at least a good one) will tell you that the conversations are anything but happy. I can't count all the Happy Hours I've spent with coworkers bashing everything from our salaries and bonuses to our benefits to the mean security guard who pretended he didn't know us even though we signed in every day.

I'm certainly dating myself with the signing-in bit, but it seems like the security in workplaces is about the only thing that has changed when it comes to Happy Hour gripes, which still include working conditions, anal bosses, dated software, go-nowhere meetings, flimsy pay, too much work demanded, and too little to show for it. This chapter not only addresses what you will never hear over the clinking of beer bottles but tells you one of the most fundamental things about your finances that your financial advisor won't tell you: *the very workplace you spend time groaning about is actually the place where most of your wealth can come from.*

In my first job as an investment banker, I worked for a great guy and a wonderful mentor whom I will call Michael. Even the Happy Hour crew gave him the thumbs-up and were jealous that I'd lucked out in getting one of the good bosses. Michael didn't always present his advice in a way that got through to me at the time, but in retrospect, I can see that he was almost always spot-on. Here is what I didn't hear him say:

**1.** I was eligible for a 6 percent match on my 401(k) plan, which meant that the company was *paying* me to invest in the plan. That match was actually larger than my raise—but I didn't even know it existed. Had Michael turned to me and said, "Davidson, do you want a 6 percent raise?" I would never have turned him down and probably would have thought he was crazy for offering. Of course I wanted a 6 percent raise! I wanted an anything-percent raise! But by not investing in my company's 401(k) plan, I was turning that raise down.

**2.** I was losing money because I had chosen the wrong health care option. Wanting to keep as much money as I could in my paycheck, I had ticked off the cheapest possible health care box—the high-deductible plan. This choice makes sense for people who are young and healthy and don't have a history of visiting doctors as often as they visit the gas station, but I did. Suffering from chronic sinusitis, I was dealing with allergies, sinus infections, or complications from sinus infections year-round and doing a lot of doctor-hopping, looking for the one who could finally make me better. On the high-deductible plan, I was paying out of pocket for the *full cost* of most of those visits (especially the out-of-network ones). I would have been better off choosing the company's more expensive plan, which would have covered a sinus surgery to fix my sinus problems for very little out-of-pocket cost. And then, after surgery had cured my sinus problems, I could have stuck with in-network doctors for annual physicals and rare illnesses. This mismanagement of my health care option cost me $30,000! Again, what would I have said if Michael had asked me, "Davidson, do you want to waste $30,000 and have a low-grade sinus infection for the next 20 years of your life, or do you want to get a fully funded operation that will fix your problems, make you healthier, and reduce your medical expenses by about 90 percent?" Do I even have to answer this question? Bottom line: to compare health care plans, don't just look at the premiums. Add in what your estimated out-of-pocket costs would be, depending on your general health. If you have an option with an HSA (health savings account), also be sure to factor in any contributions you would receive from your employer and the tax breaks you would get from your own contributions.

**3.** I worked most of my first year without realizing that, if I stayed past 8:00 P.M., the company would reimburse me for dinner and pay for my transportation home, including a car service if one was available. Once I figured it out, I pulled together as many receipts as I could find, only to discover that there was a time limit around billing—30 days from when the expense was incurred. After spending over $3,000 on dinner and transportation, I ended up with a reimbursement check for $174.92 or only about 5.8% of what I actually spent on hundreds of dinners and cab rides home after late nights at work.

**4.** My employer could have helped me with my dispute with my landlord. This was one of my favorite topics to throw a tantrum about as my coworkers and I gorged ourselves on half-price wings. I'd give him my rent check on time every month, but he would wait to cash it and then charge *me* late fees. It was criminal, but because I couldn't afford an attorney to make him stop, I chose to move out of the place, which cost me a lot in moving expenses and just overall mental anguish. Little did I know that all along my employer had offered free legal support as an employee benefit. I could have resolved this dispute by simply using that service—and maybe I could even have negotiated a lower rent in the process.

Coulda, shoulda, woulda. My experience is no different from the millions of other experiences out there that people call us about on our financial helpline. So many callers who want to work with financial advisors are looking into that option way before they have taken advantage of what is already available to them through their employer. All of these cases in which I left lots of free money on the table by neglecting to look into my employee benefits were as ludicrous as not just turning down the bread basket at a restaurant but also offering to pay the server money for it. Before working with a financial advisor, be sure you tap everything that is rightfully yours.

But there's no need to smack yourself on the forehead for not cashing in yet. It's not too late to set off on your own workplace treasure hunt! Whether you are employed by a large company that offers higher pay and richer benefits or a smaller company that offers fewer monetary incentives but more lifestyle benefits, such as flextime or free on-site day care, you can start mapping out ways to increase your wealth in your own workplace. (Just be sure to follow your company's expense policy.) To find the potential benefits that are yours for the taking in your workplace—your likeliest source of wealth-building benefits but also the place most people leave unexplored—you just need to know where to look and how to activate them.

## HOW YOUR PAYCHECK PAVES THE WAY TO WEALTH

We tend to not look under our own noses for solutions to our problems, and as I've just related, I didn't think to look to my own employer as my greatest source of wealth until I ran the numbers much later. Lured by promises of the great advantages and gains to be had on the open market, we often forget that we don't need to look any further for our wealth than our own cubicle.

Wealth begins with how much you earn and how much of that you are able to save, which is why it makes sense to start with the employer that is responsible for your earnings. Love your job or hate it, it pays you money that you can spend, save, and invest—all to the end of having a better life for yourself and your family. Your employer may be effectively paying you to take advantage of its benefits by:

- Offering to match what you invest in your 401(k) up to a certain amount. Also known as free money, this benefit has the same financial impact as an annual raise.
- Offering favorably priced group health insurance and/or paying a set amount each month into your health savings account (HSA) or health reimbursement account (HRA). HSA or HRA funds can be applied to your out-of-pocket health expenses.
- Purchasing life, disability, and long-term care insurance on your behalf. At the very least, some employers offer group pricing so that you can save money you would otherwise spend on the open market for this insurance, which you also might be unable to secure owing to preexisting health reasons.
- Negotiating discounted rates for auto and homeowner's insurance. This is a benefit some employers offer through payroll deductions. Some even offer pet insurance.

Not even included here are company profit sharing, employer stock incentives, bonuses, and financial education and advice that are free to employees and paid for by employers. Also missing from this list are the employee assistance programs (EAPs) offered by many employers. EAPs provide access to free legal support and help with substance abuse, domestic violence, or mental health issues. We are also starting to see emerging service providers that support employees in navigating the health care system to find the best doctors at the best rates.

What your financial advisor isn't telling you is that, with very rare exceptions, there's no way he or she can compete with what your employer already offers. You should *fully maximize* your employee benefits before you even consider hiring a financial advisor.

## HOW TAKING ADVANTAGE OF EMPLOYEE BENEFITS PLAYS OUT IN REAL LIFE

Sisters Kate and Emily both make $50,000 a year, save the exact same amount of money (10 percent of their salary), and use the exact same investment strategy. They even start investing on the same day. (Yes, this is hypothetical, but we see variations of it all the time.) The only difference is that Kate decides that she's going to invest the money in her company's 401(k) plan and Emily decides to use an outside advisor instead.

You would think that they will end up with the same amount of money, but flash forward 30 years: Working with her financial advisor, Emily has $460,908 in her IRA. Kate, on the other hand, has almost double that amount in her 401(k) plan—$807,278! Kate can retire from her job and live the life she's always wanted to live. Emily will have to work eight more years to attain the same level of financial security.

And all because of *where* the two sisters have invested their money— one using the services of an advisor, who puts her funds into a traditional IRA, and the other investing the same way in her employer's 401(k) plan. How is it even possible that one single decision 30 years earlier could lead to two such radically different outcomes?

Here's the story behind the story:

Kate's employer actually pays her to invest in her 401(k). By investing 6 percent or more of her salary, she gets an extra 3 percent from her employer every single year. That brings her investment total up to 13 percent of her salary versus the 10 percent that her sister invests. Kate's employer, being a very large company, also gets discount rates on those same investments—and the difference could be as much as 1.5 percent per year when we account for the fees Emily has to pay.

Emily not only has to compensate her advisor but also has to pay full retail for the mutual funds she and her advisor choose to invest in. While Kate earns a return of 8 percent each year on average—thanks in large part to the favorable pricing structure in her 401(k) and to *not* having to pay an advisor—her sister gets only a 6.5 percent return because she has to pay 1.5 percent more in fees each year. That 1.5 percent difference alone adds up to over $160,000 at the end of 30 years. The cost of Emily's "advice" comes to almost $350,000 and eight extra years of her life working in a job that she likes well enough but that is not her passion.

Sure, there are plenty of people who have it worse. But the point is that all of us can have it so much better—simply by changing the way we make seemingly simple decisions so that our money works for us, not against us.

## But That's Only Part of the Story

Keep in mind that Kate's and Emily's investments provide just one example. We have seen *hundreds* of people who ended up in Emily's situation, often when it was too late, but my hope is that we have prevented a similar scenario for thousands of others by changing the way they look at their employee benefits. It's not just your company retirement plan that you should be prioritizing. Your employer probably offers tons of other benefits, either free of charge or at a discount. Before you hire any financial advisor, find out what you have available at work and max out those opportunities.

Here we outline each of these benefits and its true financial value. You should take advantage of *all* of these benefits that make sense for you based on your financial goals and needs. Otherwise, like Emily, you could end up leaving a lot of money on the table and regretting it later.

| Company Benefit | How the Benefit Works | How to Maximize the Benefit | Estimated Financial Value of the Benefit |
|---|---|---|---|
| Company-sponsored retirement plan | Make pretax contributions that grow tax-deferred and sometimes Roth contributions that grow to be tax-free. Companies typically match your contribution with pretax funds and offer institutional investment options that may have lower expenses. | Invest at least up to the company match unless you are in dire financial straits. Beyond that, invest as much as you can. | $347,000 over 30 years.* This includes $187,000 of free money from Kate's employer (company match plus growth) and over $160,000 in additional investment earnings due to 1.5 percent lower expenses on average.<br><br>*Based on a 3 percent match on a $50,000 salary, earning an average return of 8 percent each year. |

| Company Benefit | How the Benefit Works | How to Maximize the Benefit | Estimated Financial Value of the Benefit |
|---|---|---|---|
| Investment help in the form of target date (TD) funds or a managed account option in your 401(k) plan | These tools are designed to effectively diversify your portfolio, minimizing your risk and maximizing your return. Through automatic rebalancing, these options take your emotions out of investment decisions. | Choose a TD fund when you have average risk tolerance for your age and you don't have many other outside assets, but consider a managed account option if you are more risk-averse or have large sums of outside assets. | Studies show that participants who receive investment help experience as much as a 3 percent annual performance advantage over do-it-yourself investors. |
| Health savings account (HSA) | Set aside money tax-free for out-of-pocket medical, dental, and vision expenses that comes out of your paycheck before federal, state, and FICA taxes. Requires coverage with an eligible high-deductible health plan. | Estimate your possible out-of-pocket costs to determine the minimum to contribute, but try to max out to the $3,350 individual limit* (or $6,750 family limit), since whatever you don't use rolls over for future use.  *2016 limit | Tax savings of $1,261 per year for an individual (like Kate) in the 25 percent federal tax bracket, 5 percent state tax, and 7.65 percent FICA tax. Over a 30-year career, this could add up to close to $38,000 in tax savings and almost $100,000 in earnings if the excess funds are invested year after year and earn 6 percent annually. |
| Flexible spending account (FSA) | Also enables you to set aside tax-free funds through payroll deduction for out-of-pocket medical, dental, and vision expenses. (For those eligible for an HSA, a limited-purpose FSA may only be used for vision and dental expenses.) | Since the FSA is "use it or lose," carefully estimate how much you may have in out-of-pocket expenses, up to $2,550. | Tax savings of $960 each year, or close to $29,000 over a 30-year career. |

| Company Benefit | How the Benefit Works | How to Maximize the Benefit | Estimated Financial Value of the Benefit |
| --- | --- | --- | --- |
| Wellness program incentives | Typically earn a credit toward insurance premium discount or cash incentive for participating in various wellness goals, such as taking a health risk assessment or smoking cessation. | Max out your wellness incentives by meeting all the participation requirements for a healthier you. | On average, up to a $500 wellness credit per year. |
| Discounts on diet and exercise programs | Reduced-price gym membership and Weight Watchers. | Work out at the free on-site fitness center or join the gym that offers you a group discount. | Typical discount of $10 a month could save you $120 per year on a gym membership. |
| On-site day care or discounts on day care providers | Your employer may have an agreement with a local day care provider for on-site care or off-site care at a discount (typically 10 percent). | With day care costing upward of $1,000 a month, take advantage of any discount or employer contribution available. | Discount savings of $1,200 a year on average for the five years before a child heads to school. |
| Dependent care FSA | Set aside money tax-free for day care that comes out of your paycheck before federal, state, and FICA taxes. | Since these funds are "use it or lose it," set aside no more than your estimated day care costs for the year, up to a maximum of $5,000. | Tax savings of $1,882 per year based on 25 percent federal, 5 percent state, and 7.65 percent FICA taxes. |
| Employer-paid life and AD&D (accidental death and dismember-ment) insur-ance | Typically, employers offer your beneficiaries one year's pay as a death benefit, and an additional year's pay if you die on the job accidentally. | Make sure to update your designated beneficiaries when you have a life event such as getting married or having a child. | Tax-free death benefit goes to your beneficiary. |

| Company Benefit | How the Benefit Works | How to Maximize the Benefit | Estimated Financial Value of the Benefit |
|---|---|---|---|
| Group auto/homeowner's/renter's/pet insurance | Pay for property and casualty insurance through payroll deduction, with group discounts typically around 10 percent. | Look at bundling your coverage through the group policy for maximum discount. | Average yearly savings of $466 from the group discount, according to MetLife. |
| Group short-term and/or long-term disability | Employers usually provide at least 60 percent income replacement if you suffer an extended illness or injury, with premium discounts for supplemental coverage. | Review the no-cost coverage available and add supplemental coverage if you need higher income replacement, based on your salary. | Could provide $86,500 in income replacement, based on the average of a 34.6-month long-term disability with 60 percent income replacement on a $50,000 salary. For more information, see "Chances of Disability": disability canhappen.org /chances_disability/. |
| Legal assistance | Either through a prepaid legal plan or an EAP, gain access to a free initial legal consultation and free online will preparation. | Sign up for the prepaid legal plan if you are considering buying or selling real estate or have an upcoming major life event. | Savings of around $284 per hour in average legal fees, according to RocketLawyer. |
| Tuition reimbursement | Many employers offset the cost of continuing education in your career field or help you finish a degree. | Take classes to stay up-to-date or to seek a degree in your chosen profession. | Tax-free reimbursement of up to $5,250 per year for Kate, plus being able to further her education and earn a higher paycheck. |
| Free checking account | Some companies have relationships with local banks or credit unions that offer free checking, even to employees who have had trouble in the past opening an account. | Have your paycheck direct-deposited to avoid delay in accessing your pay and to get free checking. | Avoid the average $7 monthly bank fee for a basic checking account. |

| Company Benefit | How the Benefit Works | How to Maximize the Benefit | Estimated Financial Value of the Benefit |
|---|---|---|---|
| Adoption assistance | More than half of employers now offer financial assistance toward adoption expenses. | If you are considering adopting a child, check with your HR department regarding how much paid time off would be available. | Average of $7,000 to assist with the cost of adoption and paid leave. For more information, see "More Employers Provide Adoption-Friendly Benefits": shrm.org /hrdisciplines/benefits /articles/pages/adoption -benefits.aspx. |
| Employee stock purchase plan (ESPP) | Buy your company's stock at a discount through payroll deduction. | If you would like to own stock in your employer outside of your retirement plan, consider taking advantage of this benefit. Keep in mind, however, that financial planners generally do not recommend having more than 10 to 15 percent of your overall portfolio invested in any one company, including the company you work for. | $250 savings based on a purchase of 100 shares with a stock price of $25 and a 10 percent discount. |
| Commuter tax benefits | For those who take public transit or pay for parking during the workday, pretax payroll deduction of up to $250 a month for commuting expenses and savings on federal, state, and FICA taxes. | Check with your employer for discounted public transit passes. | For a commuter with 25 percent federal, 5 percent state, and 7.65 percent FICA tax rates, savings can be up to $1,717 yearly. |

*Note:* All limits are for 2015 unless otherwise specified.

*One thing to keep in mind:* your employer may also offer a financial wellness benefit! Find out if your employer offers you the benefit of helping you make the best benefits decisions, and what type of guidance is provided. According to a study by Aon Hewitt, 93 percent of large employers provide or plan to provide some form of employee financial wellness program in 2015, and an increasing number of small and medium-sized companies are jumping on the bandwagon. This service is usually paid for in full by your employer, with no charge to you, and includes financial workshops, one-on-one financial planning sessions, and phone-based financial coaching on both your personal finances and your company benefits. Just be wary of conflicts of interest—you want access to planners who are educators, not financial services salespeople disguised as educators.

## WHAT IS FINANCIAL SECURITY WORTH TO YOU?

So now you are well ahead of where I was when I made costly benefits mistakes in the two years I worked at my first job, leaving tens of thousands of dollars on the table. You can use this as your guide to finding and securing all the "free money" your employer makes available in addition to your paycheck and walk away with much more than you expected.

The next step is on you. In addition to gaining savings from free benefits and matching dollars into your retirement plan, you have to decide how much additional money you want to sock away, using your benefits as leverage. This is a way to grow your money faster than you could with outside investment opportunities.

In a nutshell, this decision comes down to a fundamental question: how important is financial security to you? By financial security I mean the ability to do what you want in life without having to worry about being constrained by concerns about money.

Empirically, the workplace is usually where you will get the most bang for your buck. But for the 70 percent of employees who are *not* engaged in their work—those who work for a paycheck but aren't fulfilled by the work in and of itself—maximizing employee benefits is less a retirement strategy and more a strategy to get closer to pursuing their life's passion and making every single day fun, fulfilling, and even exhilarating. Or as my good friend would call it, "FU Money!"

If you're part of the majority who think "work" is a four-letter word and plan to do something about it by making a bold move, FU Money—which I term, more accurately, "Freedom Money"—can be made via your workplace benefits, and the biggest earner toward this end is your retirement plan. If you are nowhere near retirement age, or if, like me, you are lucky to fall into the minority of people who are passionate about what they do and plan to work until they die because they want to, you may find it almost impossible to relate to the idea of "retirement." None of us know, however, who (or where) we are going to be in five years, much less 35 years, so we need to redefine "retirement." I would suggest that you think about your retirement plan as *financial security for life*.

Accruing the Freedom Money to gain financial security for life means that you have saved enough to pursue your passion and live life on your own terms. This might involve working in a traditional job that's focused on an area you love but less lucrative than your current job, starting your own company, operating as a sole proprietor or independent consultant, volunteering your time for a cause that is important to you, mentoring, coaching a sports team for pay or fun, or you name it.

Freedom Money isn't for buying an island; it's for buying the *life* you want. Freedom Money gives you the freedom to walk away at any time from a position in which you've been asked to compromise your values, integrity, priorities, or self-respect. Freedom Money leads to personal and professional fulfillment and gives you that rare opportunity to find your passion, your purpose, what you were meant to contribute to the world. However idealistic this sounds, it becomes absolute reality when you have enough money to survive comfortably without a paycheck.

## HOW MUCH FREEDOM MONEY CAN YOU ACCRUE FROM MAXIMIZING YOUR EMPLOYEE BENEFITS *BEFORE* YOU HIRE AN ADVISOR?

For the most part, money isn't just going to appear for the taking out of nowhere before you've done some soul-searching, brainstorming, and planning. But as you'll see in this chapter, growing your wealth doesn't have to hurt—you can simply fund it and forget it! By automating your contributions and taking advantage of the free money available through your company benefits, including enormous savings on health care and other great perks, your needs and costs can be prioritized, manipulated, and managed over time—even in the smallest increments.

In a perfect world, we would all do whatever we want right now, but the reality is that it takes time and sacrifice to save the money to get to a place where you can live life on your own terms, completely free of financial constraints. There is one question that you—and you alone—need to consider to determine how fast you want to get to a place of financial security for the rest of your life:

> *How much money are you willing and able to save by taking advantage of free employee benefits that could replace your current expenses and also by making some sacrifices today in order to buy yourself the life you ultimately want?*

It's all about finding the right balance for you. Some people who are natural minimalists actually find the thought of shedding some of their material possessions and living a simpler life very satisfying. When it comes to possessions, I fall into this category, but don't ask me to camp instead of staying in a hotel with basic amenities or I'll panic. The last camping trip I took was in 1997—right outside the hotel we were staying at. My friend and I huddled together in a sleeping bag on the beach for about two hours and then decided to return to the hotel, which wasn't fancy but had things like heat, a bed, a bathroom, and people we could call if we ran into any problems. That is my own line in the sand, even if other people would think I'm crazy and missing out on one of the greatest joys in life.

The point is that we are all wired differently. You need to be realistic about what you can do without and what would send you into an emotional tailspin to give up. The idea is not to live in poverty today to be financially secure later in life, but rather to take advantage of the free money your employer provides, whenever you can, and then figure out what you are comfortable setting aside to get closer to living life on your own terms.

Here are three approaches we have seen people take to growing their Freedom Money.

## Level 1: The Slow but Steady Route to the "Do Whatever You Want Life"

For most people, the slow but steady approach typically requires relatively minimal changes in their lifestyle. For example, they use coupons instead of paying retail (which can become a very fun hobby for some people—watch *Extreme Couponing* on TLC if you don't believe me), cut out impulse purchases, and find great deals on vacations and entertainment.

There's a trade-off to taking this approach. It will take you longer to reach a point of full financial security where you can do what you want for the rest of your life without ever having to worry about money, but by getting there progressively, you have more freedom over time and a nice cushion if you decide you need to get out of your job, your industry, or even the workforce for a while to attend to other priorities (or figure out what you really want to do).

The slow but steady plan requires three actions:

**1.** Transferring 5 to 10 percent of your paycheck into a fund that you set aside for emergencies with the goal of being able to fund a full 12 months of living expenses from it. If you do this as an automatic transfer, through payroll or via a savings or money market account set up exclusively for this purpose, it will just happen and you won't have to think about it. Go to HR or your payroll department to obtain the forms needed to set it up. *One important note:* If you have high-interest-rate debt, you probably want to prioritize paying off that debt before building up the full 12 months' worth of living expenses, as that debt is costing you a lot more money than you will earn in interest on your emergency fund. See chapter 2 for more information on how to get out of debt.

**2.** Making sure you fully cover your health care needs. Look at your health care expenses and make sure that you've chosen a health plan based on your medical and family history, *not* just the plan with the cheapest premium. If your employer offers an HSA, contribute enough to at least cover the deductible and expected copays. If you don't spend this money, you can roll it over to the next year, and if you accumulate enough in your HSA, you can even invest this money. That way it becomes a way to not only pay for all your health care needs but actually grow your wealth over time.

**3.** Investing enough in your 401(k) plan to get your company matching funds. The most common employer matching formula is $0.50 per $1.00 up to a specified percentage (usually 6 percent). To find out your company's matching policy, go to your benefits department or benefits intranet. If your company doesn't offer a match, try to invest as close to 10 percent of your salary as you can and review this amount annually to see if you can increase it.

The following chart provides an example of how 401(k) contributions for a salary of $50,000 would grow over time using the Level 1 approach, assuming that you invest in a well-diversified portfolio designed for growth and achieve an 8 percent annualized rate of return and a company match of 3 percent of your salary when you invest at least 6 percent of your salary into the plan. This example does not account for your raises, which would automatically translate into more dollars being directed toward your 401(k).

## How Your Money Would Grow over Time with the Level 1 Approach

|  | Age 30 | Age 40 | Age 50 | Age 55 | Age 65 |
|---|---|---|---|---|---|
| Starting at age 22 | $50,201 | $180,032 | $468,212 | $725,117 | $1,678,104 |
| Starting at age 30 |  | $68,605 | $220,883 | $356,635 | $860,206 |
| Starting at age 35 |  | $27,554 | $129,764 | $220,883 | $558,885 |
| Starting at age 45 |  |  | $27,554 | $68,605 | $220,883 |
| Starting at age 50 |  |  |  | $27,554 | $129,764 |

*Note:* These numbers are based on a $50,000 annual salary with no raises included.

Please note that this example is extremely conservative, since it does not consider the following:

**1.** If you are regularly saving 5 to 10 percent of your salary, chances are that not all of what you save is going to be needed for emergencies. You should be able to direct some portion of your savings either to a fund establishing money for a down payment on a home or to your 401(k) plan once you have a fully funded emergency savings plan.

**2.** The example doesn't consider your real estate investments, including the nice amount of equity you may have in your primary residence, depending on your age and when you purchased your home and how it has appreciated over time.

**3.** The example also does not consider any inheritance you may receive or any hard assets you may have, such as jewelry, collectibles, or antiques.

**4.** The example assumes that you use all the funds in your HSA each year to pay for your medical expenses and that the account does not grow over time, but it's more likely that your HSA will grow because you will not need to use all the funds each year.

Ultimately, the goal of Freedom Money is to have enough money to pay your expenses for the rest of your life without needing to rely on a paycheck. But taking the Level 1 approach will take time.

## Level 2: Pushing on the Gas to Get to Freedom Money Faster

If financial security before retirement is your priority and you are willing and able to make more financial sacrifices—perhaps downsizing your home or getting a roommate, finding opportunities for extra income that don't interfere with your quality of life, or adopting couponing and deal hunting as a way of life—Level 2 is probably the best plan for you. Here's how it works:

**1.** Continue to direct 5 to 10 percent of your salary to a separate savings or money market account dedicated to paying for emergencies. You are going to take a slightly different approach, however, to your health care and retirement plan expenses.

**2.** If you have an HSA at work, max it out. Making the maximum contributions to your HSA may enable you not only to fund *all* of your out-of-pocket health care expenses but also to grow the account significantly over time so that it becomes a major source of wealth. The maximum you can contribute annually to an HSA as an individual in 2016 is $3,350, which is $863 more than the average American's out-of-pocket health care expenses. That difference, invested over time, can add up to hundreds of thousands of dollars. Not only that, but you get a tax deduction on all the money you set aside, and all your earnings on this money can be withdrawn tax-free if they are used for medical expenses!

**3.** Invest as much money as possible in your company's retirement plan. Start with at least 10 percent of your salary, and then automatically increase your contribution by 1 percent each year by either signing up for "auto-escalation" when you enroll in your plan or changing the percentage of your salary that you save each year.

Of all your employee benefits, with very rare exceptions, your company's sponsored retirement plan—also known, more technically, as your 401(k), 403(b), or 457 plan—is the best place to invest your savings. First of all, the money you invest in this plan is taken out of your paycheck automatically, so you don't have the chance to either spend it or proactively invest it—something that is difficult logistically and easy to forget to do. (It's also easy to rationalize skipping a payment or two . . . or 40.) Second, the money you invest is pretax, meaning that you don't pay taxes on all the money you invest in your 401(k) until you withdraw it, typically at a lower tax rate in retirement.

I can't tell you how many people Financial Finesse planners have talked to who are making around $50,000 a year and feel like they need every penny of that to survive. They understand the importance of investing 10 percent or more in their retirement plan, but can't see how they could realistically part with $5,000 per year.

Well, here's the great thing—to save $5,000 per year, most people are probably only seeing about $3,500 come out of their take-home pay, thanks to the tax break they get for investing in their 401(k) plan. That may still seem like a lot, but it's actually less than $10 per day. This is still not an easy sum of money for some people to give up, but it's a lot more doable if you use some creative strategies—carpooling, packing a lunch, finding cheaper parking, or making your own coffee.

Like Kate's company, many companies match what you invest up to a certain percentage of your salary—in other words, *the company pays you to contribute*. Kate took advantage of this benefit, and Emily could have chosen to do so too, but she didn't. The average match is about 3 percent for the first 6 percent of salary. Some companies go a step further and contribute an additional amount whether you invest or not—often based on company profits. That could amount to an extra 3 to 5 percent, or more, of free money.

And like Kate, if you defer 10 percent of your salary of $50,000 into your retirement plan (which costs you only $3,500, thanks to the tax break, but a full $5,000 still gets invested), and your company contributes 3 percent (another $1,500 per year), that's $6,500 invested in your Freedom Money fund. Think of it this way: you just purchased $6,500 with only $3,500! No financial advisor can offer you a deal like this.

### How Your Money Would Grow over Time with the Level 2 Approach

|  | Age 30 | Age 40 | Age 50 | Age 55 | Age 65 |
|---|---|---|---|---|---|
| Starting at age 22 | $98,895 | $420,875 | $1,210,376 | $1,937,807 | $4,686,078 |
| Starting at age 30 |  | $140,939 | $529,240 | $899,405 | $2,324,033 |
| Starting at age 35 |  | $50,499 | $290,834 | $529,240 | $1,465,718 |
| Starting at age 45 |  |  | $50,499 | $140,939 | $529,240 |
| Starting at age 50 |  |  |  | $50,499 | $290,834 |

*Note:* As with Level 1, this graph assumes an 8 percent annual return, but it includes HSA investments as well as 401(k) investments. The same conservatism applies as well, i.e., the impact of raises, real estate investments, other assets, and inherited money is not included. Also not included are taxes or any 10 percent penalty incurred by making an early withdrawal from retirement plan funds before age 59½. These numbers are based on a $50,000 annual salary with no raises included.

Again, take advantage of auto-escalation if your company offers it. Auto-escalation increases your contribution to your 401(k) by a certain percentage every year—typically an amount that is less than cost-of-living adjustments or the raises you might expect to receive. Most people who take this option find that their paycheck continues to grow each year while the amount they save grows as well. Auto-escalation is a win-win option and a very good one for those who are feeling strapped.

## Level 3: Treasure Island—All In for Extremely Early Retirement

There's a growing movement toward retiring extremely early—leaving the traditional workforce in your thirties or forties in order to do what you really want to do with your life. I have two former employees who followed the principles of this movement and retired at 41 and 43. Both now have their own businesses—one in software development and the other in independent films and corporate video production. Financial Finesse buys services from both, and I feel proud every time I approve those payments. These two people were meant to be entrepreneurs and were able to achieve that dream simply by going "all in."

This is Level 3, and it gets you to financial security quicker than you could probably ever imagine, but it comes with a major catch. To save enough to reach the "do whatever you want" level so you can live life on your own terms in your thirties or forties if you started early enough (within another decade or so if you started later), you will really have to cut back. For most people, this means extreme frugality—cutting out almost all the "nice to haves" in their lives and living on a budget that many of us would perceive to be relatively extreme. Obviously, this is easier to do for those with a sizable salary, but even they will find that the Level 3 approach requires that they live a much lower-key lifestyle than their peers.

To reach this level, you may need to forsake a car and find cheaper alternatives, like ridesharing, public transportation, or Uber. You also may need to forgo the standard electronics, sticking to the most basic cell plans and Internet access. Your mortgage or rent may have to get down to 10 percent of your income, which could mean living with more roommates than you would like, renting a studio apartment, or, if you are lucky, finding someone who needs a permanent houseguest to take care of their house (which can be an extra job in and of itself). You will probably need to coupon like crazy and find free forms of entertainment whenever possible.

Your friends will probably make fun of you for being "cheap," though if they are true friends, they'll respect what you are trying to do (and may even join you in the pursuit, which makes it substantially easier). Still, you may have to say no to evenings out or group trips that simply don't fit into your budget. If you have kids, you will need to involve them. Getting on board with the family's extreme budget can be incredibly empowering for kids and may help shape them into financially responsible people, but it also requires sacrifice at a time in their lives when brand names may be especially important in their social circles.

Here's how Level 3 works:

1. Do everything outlined for Level 2, with just one difference:
2. Go "all in" in your company's retirement plan.

If you are under the age of 50, you can invest up to $18,000 per year (the 2015 contribution limit) in your company's sponsored retirement plan (which really should be renamed your "Financial Security Plan," since that's what it can do for you), and if you are over 50, up to $24,000 per year. On a $50,000 salary, saving at this level can seem almost impossible because it requires putting away 60 to 70 percent or more of your *net* pay; for perspective, the average American saves less than 5 percent. But believe it or not, people have saved this much or even more, some of them making less than $50,000.

Saving at this level is technically possible, provided you don't have a large family to feed, but it is critical that you approach it as an investment and an adventure or else it will feel like extreme deprivation. Provided you don't fall into the trap of "keeping up with the Joneses," extreme saving becomes more doable as your salary grows.

Once you've grown your Freedom Money, you can take early retirement or subsidize the job of your dreams with funds from your Financial Security Plan. Just be sure to learn about how to take withdrawals while minimizing fees and taxes.

### How Your Money Would Grow over Time with the Level 3 Approach

|  | Age 30 | Age 40 | Age 50 | Age 55 | Age 65 |
|---|---|---|---|---|---|
| Starting at age 22 | $226,715 | $812,460 | $2,111,194 | $3,304,867 | $7,729,232 |
| Starting at age 30 |  | $309,789 | $996,651 | $1,645,246 | $4,049,287 |
| Starting at age 35 |  | $124,463 | $585,744 | $1,033,390 | $2,692,616 |
| Starting at age 45 |  |  | $124,463 | $346,528 | $1,169,670 |
| Starting at age 50 |  |  |  | $161,201 | $758,763 |

*Note:* As with Level 2, this graph assumes an 8 percent annual return, but it includes HSA investments as well as 401(k) investments. The same conservatism applies as well, i.e., the impact of raises, real estate investments, other assets, and inherited money is not included. Also not included are taxes or any 10 percent penalty incurred by making an early withdrawal from retirement plan funds before age 59½. These numbers are based on a $50,000 annual salary with no raises included.

Remember, the savings you can foresee is money your employer is literally *handing over to you!* Having Freedom Money doesn't require that you take a second job or downsize your house or forgo college for yourself or your children. Free money begets more free money. Over time you can experience freedom in a way that you might not have known if you had been anything like Emily and had worked with a financial advisor who didn't want to tell you to *keep your money where you make your money.*

Unfortunately, your company benefits are only one area of your financial life that a financial advisor typically doesn't tell you about or help you maximize. There's another very powerful way to become financially secure that advisors also ignore because it doesn't generate any income for them. Like your company match, directing your money toward this area of your finances will bring a guaranteed return, and one much higher than anything an advisor could reliably provide. Read the next chapter to learn more.

# 2

## Paying Off Debt:
## Your Best Investment

**Every day at** Financial Finesse, we receive calls from people who are looking "to get rich quick," usually in the form of an investment that promises a high return or a high interest rate and is completely safe — one with no chance of losing money. In all cases, either a financial advisor or a friend who has invested with a financial advisor has told the hopeful caller about some "incredible" investment, and the caller wants advice on how to take the leap to get in the game. Frankly, this kind of call always concerns me deeply.

Peter was one such caller. As a third-generation entrepreneur, Peter put his personal life on hold as he dedicated himself to growing the clientele for his catering business through marketing and by booking as many catering gigs as he could get, even the low-ball bidders. Peter's work ethic was unwavering, and he was totally dedicated to his goal, but this strategy had also resulted in a great accumulation of debt. Some of it was good debt, such as the mortgage on a property with an industrial-sized kitchen and back-door loading and unloading areas for the catering vans. But some of it was the not-so-good high-interest kind of debt. For instance, Peter had been resorting to paying his overdue bills to various vendors on his company credit card.

By springtime, Peter was feeling hopeful again: he had a slew of upcoming graduation parties and weddings in the pipeline, and his new financial advisor (a friend of his father's) had presented him with a great investment opportunity. Peter desperately needed for this opportunity to work out—it would help him grow the business while eliminating some serious credit card debt. His father had "gotten lucky" before with this advisor, and the returns seemed too attractive to pass up.

Our planners advised Peter to hold off on taking any investing chances. Fortunately, Peter was coming to the same conclusion. It wasn't long before he agreed that the promise of "instant wealth" didn't seem like a good long-term plan for growing and protecting his money so much as a greedy, unsustainable way to solve a short-term problem. Somewhere deep down, Peter's instinct was telling him there was a better and safer way to grow his business and grow his money. And he was right. What his financial advisor wasn't telling him was that paying off high-interest-rate debt is one of the best ways to guarantee high returns.

How can taking the maximum amount of cash possible and putting it toward nothing but that high-interest debt (credit card, loan, or otherwise) instead of an investment be your most profitable investment strategy?

Consider it this way. Making high returns isn't just about money; it's about how you live your life while you are making that money. If your debt is costing you the most and stifling your ability to become financially secure and independent, then it is also destroying your ability to do what you want, when you want, on your own terms—just as it did to me when I was living beyond my means in New York City. And just as Peter, instead of waiting a few years to expand his catering business into a catering hall, was spending unhappy, stressful years chained to financial institutions that were benefiting from his going-nowhere minimum monthly payments.

## YOUR LIFE AS A BUSINESS

I'm a serial entrepreneur, a business-centric type, which is probably why business concepts translate well for me to real life. When I hear stories

---

## HOW MUCH DEBT ARE YOU REALLY PAYING?

---

If you carry high-interest-rate credit cards and you simply make the minimum payment, you will likely spend much more over time in interest than the amount you charged in the first place! When I was part of this statistic, not only was I paying out serious sums every month in interest, I was losing even greater amounts in the form of income and business growth, because my debt prevented me from wisely investing in my new start-up. What I quickly learned was that paying off high-interest debt is an investment that pays you back exponentially and in many different forms beyond dollars and cents. *This is why the safest and most profitable investment is one that no advisor can make for you.* Only you can make this investment—which is to pay off your bad debt before you do anything else.

like Peter's, they remind me of how business owners handle debt—and how that can apply to all of us. Businesses measure their success in part by whether they are operating in "the black" or in "the red," terms that measure income versus expenses. The goal is to have more coming in than going out. When considering your life, I challenge you to start thinking of yourself and your financial life as a small business, with you at the helm as CEO, because when it comes to managing your wealth, the same financial rules apply. Whether you're a mom running the household full-time, a singleton on the edge of getting her master's degree, or a divorced dad with two kids, a career, and a pet iguana, your intention is no different from that of a business tycoon running a company: to run a smooth ship and operate in the black, continually growing your wealth over time.

The mind-set of business owners is accountability. Regardless of whether or not they hire accountants or financial planners to help them set and achieve their goals, business owners know that ultimately it is their responsibility to grow their own money, as they are the ones with the most to lose. Similarly, you can turn to pros for help, but when it comes to debt, I'm afraid there is no one more accountable than you.

Smart business owners know what's worth going into debt for, and they are aware that not all debt is created equal. There are types of good debt that can help them grow as well as types of bad debt that can sink them. We'll distinguish good debt from bad later in this chapter, but it's easy to remember that good debt mobilizes a person, usually in the form of real estate, small business loans, or college loans, while bad debt spins a person's wheels, like credit card debt and other "depreciating" payments, like many car payment plans.

Peter's decision to pay his vendors was a good reason to go into debt, but he wasn't aware of the options he had that would have made his debt a good debt, such as the low-interest loans or lines of credit available to him. He was using the only option he knew about—his high-interest credit cards. Interest on credit cards can skyrocket as high as 25 percent, and in Peter's case, using those cards made his good original motive to pay off his debt into a bad decision in the end.

For the most part, we find ourselves in one of three categories at any given point in our lives:

1. The **Financiers** use good debt to grow wealth.
2. The **Frustrated** are struggling with high-interest-rate debt but still managing to stay afloat.
3. The **Free Fallers** are in serious trouble with debt and need to take immediate corrective action to restore their finances.

We can, and often do, move from one category to another over the course of our lives. Our Financial Finesse planners have seen thousands of people recover from nearly bankrupt conditions to become financially independent—able to sustain themselves financially for the rest of their lives. Similarly, I'm sure all of you reading this book know people who took on what is typically considered "good" debt to grow their wealth, like mortgages and student loans, only to find themselves in significant financial trouble when the mortgage crisis and recession hit in 2008–2009. We started working with many of these people when they were totally overwhelmed with debt at that time, and now they are back on their feet again and have gone back to building wealth. *Bottom line:* there is absolutely no reason that your past has to be your future. Being in debt can be painful or even devastating, but in all cases you can make sure that it's only a *temporary* condition.

All that being said, chances are that you fit into one of these categories right now in terms of how you manage your debt. Whether you're a Financier, among the Frustrated, or a Free Faller, this chapter will help you make debt your best overall "investment" by showing you how to pay off the high-interest-rate debt from credit cards that is currently destroying your wealth. You will also learn how to grow your wealth by using low-interest-rate debt ("good" debt) to secure investments in your future and ultimately become financially independent and secure.

**The Financiers:** Financiers are people who are lucky enough to have only debts that they have taken on deliberately in order to finance growth. For example, when I was young, in the mid-1970s, my dad was relocated for work and my parents had to move from Ohio to Southern California. They made an incredibly smart decision at that time, as did a few other families in our neighborhood. They chose to buy a house in a quiet, low-key community that was safe and had good schools but was virtually unknown, even by those who already lived in Los Angeles.

For what would be considered a modest mortgage by today's standards, they and other families purchased homes in the neighborhood—mostly unremarkable suburban homes—with the hope that the real estate values would appreciate over time. The place is much better known today—Palos Verdes, California. Home to Trump National Golf Course, the five-star luxury resort called Terranea, and some of the most breathtaking real estate in Southern California. On average, the families in our neighborhood put $10,000 to $20,000 down on mortgages to purchase their homes and ended up selling them for between $2 million and $4 million about 20 years later, when their homes were nearly or completely paid off. That's a nice retirement nest egg by anyone's standards!

Another example of the Financier is the business owner who uses working capital or takes out Small Business Administration (SBA) loans to add a fleet of trucks to a booming warehouse business or does what virtually every business does at some point to finance its growth—purchases overstock inventory or borrows start-up capital or capital for expansion that would otherwise have to be delayed until enough cash is generated. This type of good debt not only is okay but, if managed properly, fuels the growth of wealth.

Yet another example is the high school graduate who takes out a college loan to go to a good college, with plans to become an investment banker, a consultant, and ultimately a high-ranking company executive. Yes, the education is expensive, but the pedigree, contacts, and head start it provides are invaluable. Like the mortgages taken out by my parents and their neighbors in Palos Verdes 40 years ago, the return on investment from a good education can be absolutely astounding based on the long-term income potential.

Even a car, if needed for work, can be well worth the debt. One of our planners took on a low-interest-rate auto loan to purchase a car for a job marketing insurance to financial planning firms all over the state of Pennsylvania. Her success ultimately led her to become financially independent and secure. This success story was one of the key reasons we hired her; she had walked the walk with her own finances, so we knew she would be effective helping others do the same.

**The Frustrated:** The vast majority of Americans, the ones in the middle, are winging it. They aren't on the verge of bankruptcy, but they do use high-interest debt to finance purchases—not to make investments—and that eats into their ability to invest in their future. They typically pay double-digit interest rates for this privilege, sometimes as high as 15 to 25 percent, and often they have other debts as well.

The Frustrated find themselves in a precarious situation of trying to get by from paycheck to paycheck. If they suddenly lose their main source of income or if an unexpected disaster occurs, they can quickly fall into the next category.

**The Free Fallers:** In our experience as financial educators, most people, at some point in their lives, slip into free fall with their debt. In the beginning, free fall is fun. It's like you are strapping yourself in for an out-of-control thrill ride at a theme park, and there's a rush to the whole experience. The problem is, before you blink twice, the ride ends and you are at rock bottom, head still spinning. Financial free fall is pervasive in our society, and it's a mistake many people find themselves making. Millions are seduced by the lure of credit cards, only to wake up to the hangover of owing too much money. And even though the credit cards require only a minimum payment each month, what too few people realize is that high interest rates are sending them down a pathway of never getting out of debt.

But here's some good news. If you are tired of being financially frustrated or in financial free fall, the truth is that *as little as a few dollars a day* could send you from struggling financially to becoming financially secure and independent! It's crazy how big an impact small changes can have, and realizing this is probably the only good thing about high-interest-rate debt. The fact is that by paying even just a little more than the minimum payment, you can get out of debt faster than you ever imagined.

In truth, no one in the financial services industry ever tells you this, but thinking and doing things just a *little* differently can change your financial picture. Credit card companies don't want you to know that, financial advisors are focused on what you have to invest and not on what you owe, no merchant is going to ask you if you really can afford those designer sunglasses or that nice dinner out, and no private school for your children will tell you that you can't afford the tuition.

In short, before you can start to accumulate wealth, you need to first take care of unwanted debt. And as noted, this is not the kind of advice that financial advisors usually give you.

## THE DEBTBLASTER STRATEGY:
## HOW $3 A DAY PAYS DOWN DEBT

If you're winging your expenses with the help of credit card debt at high interest rates, then the DebtBlaster Strategy was designed with you in mind.

Paying off high-interest debt may feel like an exercise in futility, especially if you're making minimum payments each month and continuing to charge new purchases the next month. You feel unable to get ahead or worse, like you are slowly sinking into quicksand as you watch your balance grow when you just want all the debt to go away. Credit card interest rates vary, but in most economic environments today they average 15 to 25 percent a year. In contrast, the best-performing investments—stocks or equity mutual funds—have returned an average annualized return of about 10 percent per year over the course of time, with absolutely no guarantee and some very negative years along the way. Just imagine how much better off you would be financially if you got rid of that high-interest credit card balance.

Once we explained to Peter how all this looks long term, he decided to make his debt work for him and to put his financial advisor's investment on the back burner. Using the DebtBlaster Strategy, Peter was able to visualize how even the smallest and slowest debt reduction habits could greatly improve his business and his life.

Here's how the strategy works. Imagine you have two possible futures. In one future, you worry about it later—you don't add to your debt, but you continue to make just the minimum monthly payment on the debt. In your alternate future, you make a very simple but life-changing decision. On top of your minimum payment, you pay an extra $3.33 per day (which comes to $100 per month) toward your debt on your credit card with the highest interest rate. When that card is paid off, you then put those monthly payments toward the card with the next-highest interest rate and repeat the cycle until your debt is down to zero.

Just as a tunnel is cut through a mountain with a blast from one stick of dynamite at a time, this slow and steady strategy blasts debt, which is why we named it the DebtBlaster Strategy. It has changed the lives of many, many people.

By using the DebtBlaster Strategy as detailed in the chart below, you're able to pay off credit card debt of $15,000 and become debt-free in less than five years, as opposed to *over 24 years* by just making the minimum payment—and you save more than $24,000 in interest! And as we advised Peter, once you pay off your debt you can invest that $340 a month at, say, an average 7 percent rate of return—for an additional savings of more than $150,000 by the time you would have finally become debt-free making minimum payments.

# DebtBlaster Calculator

Making extra payments on your debt is a surefire way to pay it off faster. See how much faster using this DebtBlaster strategy.

## Your Debt Accounts

| Account Name | Current Balance | Interest Rate | Minimum Payment | Lump Sum Payment | Monthly Payments | Months to Pay Off |
|---|---|---|---|---|---|---|
| Credit Card 1 | $7,500 | 19% | $120 | $0 | $220 | 50 |
| Credit Card 2 | $7,500 | 7% | $120 | $0 | $120 | 78 |
| Add Account | | | | | | |

| | |
|---|---|
| Total Balance on All Accounts (Total Debt) | $15,000 |

## Additional Contribution Amounts

| New Lump Sum | New Monthly Amount | Total Monthly Payment |
|---|---|---|
| $0 | $100 | $340 |

## DebtBlaster Strategy Estimate

| | Minimum Payments Only | With DebtBlaster Strategy |
|---|---|---|
| Total Years Until Debt Free | 24 years 3 months | 4 years 11 months |
| Total Estimated Cost of Debt | $44,222 | $20,043 |
| Total Estimated Interest | $29,222 | $5,043 |
| Total Interest Saved | | $24,179 |

### Total Months Until Debt Free

DebtBlaster Strategy
Minimum Payments Only

months

59
291

0    50    100    150    200    250    300    350

The following five-step strategy for getting out of debt, used in con-junction with the DebtBlaster Strategy, can make a dramatic difference in your financial situation in a relatively short period of time. Remember I said that your past doesn't need to be your future? This five-step strat-egy is one key reason why.

---

### NO CREDIT WHERE CREDIT IS DUE

High-interest-rate debt not only costs a lot but is generally used to fi-nance expenses that lose value either immediately or over time. Charge that pair of Cole Haan leather driving gloves for the boss's birthday gift at $118.00, and you'll have to resell those gloves for $147.50 just to break even on the interest of 25 percent. It's a pretty safe bet, though, that a pair of gloves that the boss sweats in and stretches out and then sits on will not appreciate by $29.50. It's a bad investment! At the end of the day, you have very little or nothing to show for what you pur-chased, and even worse, you most likely didn't get a job promotion ei-ther. This kind of debt is not just bad but toxic, because it destroys your wealth instead of enabling you to grow it.

---

## FIVE STEPS TO GET OUT OF HIGH-INTEREST-RATE DEBT

### Step 1: Cut up your credit cards.

The only way to stop accumulating debt is to stop swiping your credit card. Cut up the cards and rely on the money you have to buy the things you need. Yes, this may be painful, but at some point a sense of self-discipline comes into play.

However, keep your debit card handy. Debit cards are as good as cash because they deduct money directly from your bank account every time you make a purchase. Obviously, if you don't have the money in your ac-count, your debit card will keep you from spending more money. (Be

---

### CANCELING ACCOUNTS?

---

This is important. Don't mistake cutting up your credit cards for canceling the accounts. That will not help you when it comes to your credit score. In fact, closing a credit card account can actually lower your score and be detrimental to your qualifications when it comes time to make a big-ticket move, like applying for a mortgage or car loan. So again, you can and should destroy your credit cards, but do not cancel your credit card accounts.

---

sure to ask your bank to turn off overdraft capabilities.) Again, this is discipline in action.

## Step 2: Negotiate with the credit card companies.

So many people are shocked when we tell them to call their credit card companies and simply ask to negotiate their interest rates. They're surprised because these companies aren't advertising the fact that it is in their best interest to keep you paying off at least some of your debt rather than defaulting on all of it. They also tend to be very receptive to reducing the interest rate on your credit card, especially if you let them know you have offers at lower rates from other credit card companies.

Here's a suggestion: try to transfer your credit card balances to one or two cards with a very low interest rate. Some cards offer introductory interest rates as low as 0 percent, but be sure to read the fine print. That rate usually lasts for only a short period of time, typically about 12 months, and then jumps up to a much higher rate. But the DebtBlaster Strategy, coupled with just 12 months of borrowed time by transferring your balance to a card that charges (temporarily) 0 percent interest, can make a huge difference. Just make sure you check carefully as to when and how high the rate will reset after the introductory period so that you can mark your calendar and are not putting yourself in an even worse position over the long term.

## Step 3: Consider a loan.

Sometimes borrowing money at a lower interest rate to pay off your high-interest-rate credit cards and loans makes sense. This strategy is often known as consolidating your debts. But if you use it, commit to doing so just once, as it's only a temporary fix. Plus, you could be putting your financial security at risk in the long term, particularly if you take out a home equity loan and then default. If you decide to go this route, here are some options, from least expensive to most expensive:

*A Home Equity Loan or Home Equity Line of Credit*
**Pros:** The interest rate tends to be very low and is tax-deductible. A 4 percent interest rate can be 3 percent net of the tax deduction if you're in the 25 percent tax bracket and you itemize your deductions.
**Cons:** You may be putting your home on the line if you can't make your monthly payments.

*A Loan from Your 401(k) Retirement Plan*
**Pros:** There's no credit check and all the interest payments go back into your own account.
**Cons:** This loan usually has to be paid back over five years, so the payments, which are taken right out of your paycheck, could be higher. Also, if you leave the company or are terminated, you typically must pay back the balance of the loan in 30 to 60 days (which can add to your financial pressures). Anything you don't pay back is considered a withdrawal from your 401(k) and subject to income tax plus a 10 percent penalty if you're under age 59½.

*A Peer-to-Peer Lending Loan*
> **Pros:** The interest tends to be lower than you can get with a personal loan from a bank.
> **Cons:** The rate is still highly dependent on your credit score, so it might not be that much lower than what you're paying now.

*Peer-to-Peer Lending Sites*

Peer-to-peer lending sites such as prosper.com, lendingclub.com, and karrot.com allow people to loan to and borrow from other people over the Internet. Although it can be risky to be a loaner, borrowers may be able to get lower interest rates than they would from a bank. If you use one of these sites, they will check your credit history and debt-to-income ratio. Including personal information in your application about who you are and why you need the money might be more likely to elicit a positive response from an individual lender than from a financial institution.

## Step 4: Fully unleash your DebtBlaster Strategy by becoming a minimalist.

Determine the expenses you can cut, with a focus on those whose elimination will actually enhance your quality of life. Does your workplace have a gym, or do you enjoy exercising with friends—running, walking, yoga, even dancing? Cancel the gym membership. Do you watch only certain shows on TV? Watch them on a streaming service like Netflix and cancel your cable subscription. Are you an environmentalist when it comes to recycling but not very conscious of your electricity consumption? Use energy-efficient lightbulbs and set the thermostat down a little lower. Love coffee? Buy your own and brew it—you'll save a couple of dollars a day, not to mention saving on the gas you've been using to drive to the nearest coffee shop. Finally, go online and stop any and all automatic payments for the services you've decided you no longer need.

To figure out how you are spending your money, use a website or mobile app that tracks and categorizes your spending for you for free, such as Mint or YodleeMoneyCenter. You might be surprised by the number of expenses you can cut or eliminate once you see how you spend your money each month!

Just by canceling her landline, cable, and gym membership (none of which she was using), Lara was able to increase her minimum credit card payment by $100 a month. With an interest rate of 20 percent on her $6,500 balance and an original minimum monthly payment of $110, it would have taken her 21 years to pay off her debt. By making monthly payments of $210 and consolidating her balance to a card that had a 0 percent interest rate and waived all interest on purchases and balance transfers for a full year, she was able to get out of debt in less than 3 years versus the 21 years it would have taken her otherwise. Even more significant, she saved over $20,000 in interest!

Take the money you have saved by eliminating expenses and apply it to your credit card with the highest interest rate. Set up an automatic monthly transfer to ensure that you stick to your plan—and to reduce your own stress. When that card is paid off, take the full amount you were paying on it and set up automatic monthly payments on the card with the next-highest interest rate. Repeat until your last card is paid off.

## Step 5: Build up an emergency fund.

The roof has a leak, the car needs to be taken to the shop, or you're between jobs. This is where a general emergency fund comes in. Did you know that charging the costs associated with emergencies on credit cards is the number one reason those who get out of debt end up back in it?

You don't want to be like Rob, whose HVAC system broke completely in the middle of the worst winter on record. With a young family, he had no other choice but to charge a new one on his credit card. At 20 percent compounding interest, that $5,000 HVAC incurred $83 of interest over the course of just one month. That was bad news by year's end.

Take your next bonus, gifts from family or friends, money you make selling items on eBay, or any supplemental income you earn, *and put it in a separate account that you can't easily access.* Deposit this money, for instance, in a money market account, a CD, or a savings account at a different bank than where you keep your checking account. Think twice before getting an ATM card for this money or setting up an online account. The more inconvenient it is to access, the less you'll be tempted to use it for non-emergency purchases.

Set a goal to build your emergency fund to cover the cost of your necessary expenses for three to six months. If you have an unstable job or a big family to support, up to 12 months is recommended. But the important thing is to start somewhere. Even one month is better than no months, until you pay off your high-interest-rate cards. With an emergency fund, you won't be forced to use your credit cards to pay for a true emergency.

Just as Lara was able to accomplish her goals by following these steps (in the right order), most people can be completely debt-free in one to three years. Even better, by year four they too can start building wealth instead of chasing after it!

## USE GOOD DEBT WISELY TO GROW YOUR WEALTH

After all this discussion of how to climb out of debt, it may be difficult to imagine that debt can actually be used as a driver for building wealth.

I personally had a strong aversion to debt, as did my husband, Joe, after our respective experiences with debt years before we even met. The prospect of getting into debt again to purchase a home just felt wrong, even though we were on strong financial footing at that point and, ironically, I was running a financial education company and teaching others about the power of good debt! Fortunately, we took the leap after some serious number crunching, and buying a house ended up being a very smart move. In fact, we were able to sell the home at a profit just two years later—netting a sizable amount even after we paid off the mortgage, taxes, and a few home repair costs.

Joe used the profit we made to start a business purchasing, refurbishing, and selling classic cars (the only kind that *does* appreciate over time). Not only is the business profitable and growing, but Joe is being paid to do what he considers his favorite hobby! It doesn't get better than that.

*Important note:* Before you take on *any* good debt to invest in your future, make sure that you can afford the payments. You also need to make sure that what you are purchasing with the debt is highly likely to appreciate in value over time.

## Examples of Good Debt

*Real Estate*
When it comes to a safe long-term investment, chances are good that your financial advisor will not steer you in the direction of real estate unless he or she also has a license to sell real estate.

Think of what would happen if mortgages were not available. Most Americans would not be able to afford a home—at least not one they would actually enjoy living in. Instead, they would pay rent for decades with nothing to show for it. In short, they wouldn't build up any equity. Alas, only the landlords would benefit.

A mortgage is considered a good debt to take on for many reasons:

**1.** Interest rates are marginal compared with the rates of the 1980s and are much lower than credit card rates.

**2.** Real estate values have been historically less volatile than the stock market.

**3.** There are tax benefits to paying interest on a mortgage that can help increase the amount of your annual tax refund, which then can be put to good use (such as paying off high-interest debts, saving for college, or even paying down the mortgage).

Financial institutions provide mortgages so that people can borrow most of the money needed to pay for their house. Interest rates for mortgages are typically fairly low, and because the interest you pay is tax-deductible, the net rate is even lower than what is stated on your mortgage documents! Provided you can comfortably afford the amount of your mortgage and pay for other house-related expenses (upkeep, insurance, and so on), you are not throwing your money away as you are with rent. Instead, you are paying down the loan so that when the time comes to sell the house, there is less you have to pay back to the bank and more to keep for yourself.

The key here is *being able to afford the mortgage*—and to be able to pay it comfortably. The 2008–2009 mortgage crisis resulted from people getting mortgages they simply couldn't afford when interest rates increased. You should never pay more than 36 percent of your monthly take-home pay on a mortgage payment. If you have a variable mortgage where rates change over time, you should look at your highest possible mortgage payment when you do this calculation.

*Small Business Loans*
Small business is actually big. The 23 million small businesses in America account for 54 percent of all US sales. Additionally, small businesses provide 55 percent of all jobs and have created 66 percent of all new jobs since the 1970s, according to the Small Business Association. The impressive 600,000-plus franchised small businesses in the United States account for 40 percent of all retail sales and provide jobs for some 8 million people. The small business sector in America occupies 30 to 50 percent of all commercial space—an estimated 20 to 34 billion square feet. It's no wonder small business loans surpassed $19 billion in 2014!

Small business loans are a good type of debt, as long as they are not secured by personal assets and their interest rates are reasonable. (The Small Business Administration is a great resource for finding out what's reasonable). These loans can help you get your business off the ground. Millions of successful small businesses were started with small business loans and would not be around today without this important source of capital. More recently, crowdfunding sites like kickstarter .com and kiva.com, and specialty sites for online merchants like kabbage.com have been great sources of credit for aspiring entrepreneurs.

*Student Loans*
Student loans can be good debt, but with the following stipulations:

**1.** You've tapped out grants and scholarships and, if you are working, you've used the full education funding available through your job.
**2.** You have fully examined the amount of the loan in light of the increased earnings you are likely to receive as a result of securing the degree in your field of choice. Far too often student loans are "upside down"—you pay a lot of money to get a degree in the humanities from an expensive private school only to discover that job openings for your major are sparse and low-paying.

One tip on student loans for those pursuing undergraduate degrees: there's nothing wrong with going to a community college or state school for a couple of years to save money and then transferring to a higher-rated college for the final two years. This can dramatically reduce the amount of student loans you need to carry.

*Car Loans*
Like student loans, car loans can be good debt, but only under certain conditions. Obviously, you need a car loan if your life simply cannot "work" without a car and you can't pay for it in cash. Look for the lowest interest rate possible. If the loan is at or close to 0 percent and you

are disciplined about making regular loan payments, car loans can be a lifesaver. You might even get a good rate from the dealer to help close the sale. Otherwise, your bank or credit union might give you a better deal.

A car loan becomes bad debt when you purchase a car you can't afford and end up with payments that eat up your cash flow and put you back into credit card debt. It can also happen if you purchase a second car you can't afford and don't really need.

## WHAT TO DO IF YOU'RE IN FINANCIAL FREE FALL

When Allison called our financial helpline, she was frustrated. She admitted that she had made plenty of mistakes that got her into a high-interest debt bind, but she also shared that she had made what she thought were some positive moves to reduce her debt. Yet her debt just seemed to linger. "It seems I can never catch up," she said, "and I just feel like it's hopeless. I'm totally tired of living this way."

Playing catchup is one of the most common scenarios we hear. When you pay off your car loan and finally own the title, only to have the transmission blow the next day, where's the justice? It's enough to steer people away from their DebtBlaster Strategy and treat themselves to a DebtBinge instead. They just keep spending what they don't have because "what's the difference anyway!"

But remember what I said earlier—your financial past does not have to be your future. Debt is a temporary condition, and everyone can ultimately pay down, settle, or discharge their debts and transition to building wealth. Our planners let Allison know this; they recognized that her despair was holding her back as much as the state of her finances. Even if you feel like you can't possibly scrape a single extra dollar from your budget to make the minimum payments on your debt, there are *still* ways to get out of debt.

It comes down to a four-step process:

**1.** Prioritizing

**2.** Negotiating

**3.** Improving your financial situation

**4.** Using credit counseling or bankruptcy to settle or discharge your debts so that you can start over (but only if necessary, because taking this step affects your credit score)

## Step 1: Prioritize your debts.

Taking into consideration the fact that not all debt is considered equal, what you now know about good debt and bad debt will help you prioritize your debt in the order in which you are going to attack it. The following list shows how to prioritize your debts when you are overextended and can't pay all of them down.

**Priority #1—Secured debts:** Staying current with payments on secured debts like your mortgage (including property taxes and homeowner's insurance) and your car loan should be your first priority because you can lose your home or your car if you don't pay them. If you don't want to be the subject of a future *Repo Men* episode, make sure you're caught up on these first.

**Priority #2—Back taxes:** As you would probably expect, the IRS (and state tax collection agencies) have some tricks up their sleeves when it comes to collecting on back taxes, including seizing your assets and garnishing your wages. It's also very difficult to discharge tax debt in bankruptcy.

**Priority #3—Student loans:** Unless you are eligible for a forbearance or deferment, it's a good idea to make payments on these next. Like the IRS, the banks or collection agencies holding your student loan debt can take your tax refunds and garnish your wages to satisfy the debt. Student loans are hard to discharge in bankruptcy, and if you default, you can also lose the ability to get other federal loans, whether for school or housing.

**Priority #4—Payday loans:** Payday loans are not secured by assets that can be seized, but they have astronomical interest rates and are deducted from your paycheck on payday (hence the name). If being late on your mortgage and/or car payment for one month would help you pay off your payday loan, it may be better to do so in order to get rid of the sky-high finance costs of the payday loan. Typically, being just one month behind on secured debt won't trigger a repossession.

**Priority #5—The rest of your unsecured debt:** This is most likely to be credit card debt and medical debt that hasn't passed the statute of limitations yet. There are a few things to keep in mind here. Obviously, interest rates are important in determining which payments to make, as high-interest-rate debt is more expensive than lower-interest-rate debt, and the last thing you need when you are in debt trouble is a rapidly growing high-interest-rate debt that puts you even further behind. It's also important to know that older delinquencies don't hurt your credit as much as newer ones, so try to keep current with your newer debts first. Second, medical debt doesn't hurt your credit as much as other debt, so it might be a lower priority, but be aware that you may not be able to see a particular doctor again until your debt is squared away.

If you have an old debt that you haven't paid on in a while, check to see if your state's statute of limitations, which usually ranges from three to six years, has passed. If so, there's not much the creditor can do to you, and after seven years it will fall off your credit report. But be careful: if you make a payment or sometimes even if you just acknowledge the debt, the seven-year clock can restart. Even if it's still on your credit report, it won't hurt your credit as much as a new delinquency will.

Once you know what your financial priorities are, you can go on to Step 2.

## Step 2: Try to restructure your debt or negotiate an affordable payment plan with your creditors.

**Mortgage debt:** Contact the federal government's Making Home Affordable Program at 888-995-HOPE to discuss your options with a HUD-approved housing counselor.

**Tax debt:** Contact the IRS or your state revenue agency and see if you can arrange to pay the debt in installments. If not, you can try to negotiate an "offer in compromise" with the IRS to settle the debt for less than you owe.

**Student loans:** Contact your loan servicer and see if you can switch to a payment plan with lower payments, postpone the payments through deferment or forbearance, or even have the debt canceled or forgiven if you work in certain occupations.

**Other debt:** Call your creditors and ask if they would be willing to negotiate a payment or settlement plan with you. Let them know you're trying to avoid bankruptcy, which would be the worst-case scenario for them. They'd prefer to get something rather than nothing.

Austin is a great example: his lender settled his delinquent truck loan of over $8,000 for a lump-sum payoff of just $2,000 after learning that the engine was blown on his pickup. Send your responses by certified mail and keep copies of all correspondence in writing, especially the details of any deal you reach with your creditors, including their agreement to report the debt as paid or settled in full on your credit report.

If you still fall short of being able to pay your bills even after negotiating with your creditors, consider making some of the changes in step three to improve your financial situation.

## Step 3: Avoid bankruptcy by improving your financial situation.

**Generate additional income:** Taking on a second job can be unpleasant, particularly if you are already working full-time, but it can make a significant difference. The same can be said for when a stay-at-home spouse reenters the workforce temporarily to bring in extra money.

**Sell assets:** For most people, selling assets is less unpleasant, especially if they focus on selling assets that have no impact on their day-to-day life. It never ceases to surprise me how many sellable things are gathering dust in people's garages and attics—extra cars, motorcycles, boats, ski gear, snowmobiles, art, jewelry, antiques, and collections of just about anything. A godsend for people who want to generate relatively quick cash is eBay, where you can sell what you need to sell to someone who is looking for just that item.

**Change your lifestyle without sacrificing your sanity or your family's safety:** This is the most difficult option, and it's a decision you really have to consider carefully. If you are living very modestly already, downsizing might not even be possible. It's also important to consider your children and elderly parents and make sure that you are not putting them in a difficult situation by cutting back. That said, there are ways to cut lifestyle expenses that can actually enhance your quality of life.

For example, if you have an extra room in the house, you might be able to rent it to a trusted friend or family member who could contribute a few hundred extra dollars a month to your income. Better yet, get rid of the extra room by downsizing and reducing your rent or mortgage payment. Consider cheaper transportation options, couponing (which can sometimes reduce costs for groceries and other staples to close to zero), and making inexpensive meals at home instead of dining out. Get resourceful and creative without cutting things that will compromise your safety or peace of mind.

If you try all of the above and still are unable to pay the minimum payments on your debt, there's one last step to consider.

## Step 4: Seek credit counseling or bankruptcy.

Credit counseling agencies can help you settle your debts, often for a fraction of what you owe. It's also a necessary step before you can file for bankruptcy protection.

Be careful, though, because there are lots of scams out there preying on the unwary. Avoid debt settlement companies and look instead for nonprofit credit counseling agencies from reputable organizations like the National Foundation for Credit Counseling and the Association of Independent Consumer Credit Counseling Agencies. Credit counseling and bankruptcy will be reported on your credit report and temporarily damage your credit. However, when you consider the impact of not being able to pay your bills, getting rid of your debts gives you the ability to start over and rebuild. Over time you are likely to end up with a better credit score, provided you manage your future debt wisely.

## HOW TO STAY DEBT-FREE

I define a debt-free life as having no debt that is draining your wealth rather than adding to it. You have no credit card debt, no payday loans to pay off, and no other high-interest-rate debt that you use primarily to finance purchases rather than investments. A debt-free life does *not* require that you rent a home forever instead of taking out a mortgage, or forgo a college education because you don't want to take out a student loan. You should be a Financier when the time and circumstances are right.

The problem most people face after they get out of credit card or other high-interest-rate debt is figuring out how to stay out of it. Usually, the downward spiral starts with an emergency or even an increase in

income, which can lead you to upgrade your lifestyle. The problem is
that spending more for this reason is a slippery slope and people often
don't even realize they're getting into trouble until it's too late. We have
an amazing ability to rationalize:

"When I get my bonus, I'll pay off my debt."

"The emergency wasn't something I could have planned for, so it
doesn't really count."

"My career is going so well that I can live a larger lifestyle because I
know I'll be able to pay off my credit card balances pretty soon."

If you find yourself with thoughts like these—stop. Such thoughts
are major warning signs. It's the same kind of thinking we do when we
break a diet ("I'll have a cookie just this once," "I'll exercise more tomor-
row," "I still fit into some of my clothes . . ."), and it is usually the beginning of a problem that becomes much bigger.

The key to staying out of debt is to *commit* to a financially healthy
lifestyle. This means:

**1. Living within your means:** Track your budget through online
tools like Mint and make sure that you're in the black—earning more
than you spend.

**2. Paying with your debit card or cash whenever possible:**
Avoid racking up credit card charges.

**3. Having a plan B:** Create a strong emergency fund so that when
emergencies happen, you can pay for them with cash.

**4. Automating your life:** Pay your bills automatically, in full,
through online bill-pay. Set up your emergency savings fund by automatically transferring a percentage of your paycheck to a separate account.

**5. Removing the need for willpower:** Don't torture yourself with
temptation. Studies show that willpower is actually a limited resource,
and the best thing we can do when we want to become healthier
financially and physically is to simply remove temptation.

Depending on how you currently manage your finances, these steps may sound dubiously simple or overwhelming and unrealistic. The good news is that becoming financially healthy is a process; you will get better at it as you go along. And ultimately, like anything in life that we practice regularly, it will become a habit—the way you live your life.

Even better, it will lead you to a place you might never have imagined was even possible—financial security and independence for yourself and your family.

One final note: after you recover from debt and shift into building wealth, you'll most likely get to a point where it is time to hire a financial advisor. Read on to learn how you can spot a bogus advisor—or bogus advice—so you can avoid becoming either a victim of fraud or its unfortunate side effect, eschewing good financial advice when you really need it.

# 3

## Beware of Bogus Advisors

**Before you read on,** please read the important message below. You do yourself a disservice if you don't. This chapter is dedicated to helping you spot and avoid fraudulent or negligent advisors. They are definitely out there, and they are a risk to your financial security, as all the investors in Bernie Madoff's fund found out that fateful day in 2008 when his Ponzi scheme was exposed. However, I don't want to discourage you from using an advisor if you have money you want to invest outside your company benefits and if you want to put together a strong financial plan to invest and protect that money so that it will grow in line with your goals. A good financial advisor can be a tremendous help and can accelerate how quickly you build wealth in a way that fits your personal financial situation and goals.

To completely eschew using an advisor can be as big a mistake as picking the wrong one, since studies show that investors who don't get investment advice typically generate much lower returns than those who do. A recent study by Financial Engines and Aon Hewitt showed that those who had investment help earned over three percentage points more on average per year than those who did not. That translates into almost 80 percent more wealth over 20 years. If you are looking for an advisor, I urge you to focus on chapter 8, which will tell you not only how to find an advisor but how that person can help you.

Think of it this way—we've all heard horror stories about doctors who made terrible mistakes or committed gross malpractice, but that doesn't mean that we refuse to get medical help when we need it. The same applies to financial advisors. When you need financial advice, they can be a tremendous help—it's just a matter of finding the best one for your situation (and being able to spot the Bernie Madoffs of the world before you hand over your life savings).

John worked hard all his life, climbing the corporate ladder rung by rung, scrimping and saving to support his family so that his wife could devote her time to raising their four children, who were thriving. John's career was going well, and he was expecting to be able to retire early and devote his time to mentoring young people.

At just 51, John gave notice to his employer, hired a highly successful financial advisor, and took the advisor's advice to roll over his 401(k) balance into an IRA and invest in some "alternative investments" that were available only to high-net-worth investors. With just over $4 million in his 401(k) plan and some outside investments he had made on his own, John was just such an investor. He paid for his first child's tuition to UC Berkeley so that she wouldn't have to take out a single student loan, and he promised his three other kids that he would pay for them to attend any college or university they wanted.

And then, five years later, the bottom fell out. John's family lost everything.

John turned on his TV to see his financial advisor being arrested for running a Ponzi scheme. After making some frantic phone calls, he discovered that this person had raided his account, along with the accounts of hundreds of other investors. There was nothing left. The financial statements John had been receiving had all been falsified, and distributions that he had taken from his account had actually been paid for by newer investors who had also invested their hard-earned savings with the advisor.

There's a proverb: "It takes 50 years to build a reputation, and just 50 seconds to lose it." By anyone's standards, John had done everything right for most of his life when it came to his finances, so much so that he was teaching others how to follow in his footsteps. His finances were disastrously derailed, however, by one single bad decision that had seemed like a no-brainer at the time—to hire an advisor widely known for his ability to achieve consistently high returns, quarter after quarter.

That one single act of hiring the wrong advisor wiped out all John's hard work, all his good decisions, and virtually every single dollar he had to his name. One single act erased John's ability to fund college educations for three of his four children. One single act put John in a position where he had to look for work during the recession, at age 56 after five years of retirement. One single act forced him to sell his home, downsize to a much smaller house in a rougher neighborhood, and ask his wife to look for employment.

When you think about it, it's amazing how much control financial advisors have over our lives. Choose one who is actually a criminal, and it is possible to lose your entire nest egg along with all the hopes and dreams that went along with it. This kind of financial devastation has ruined many people's lives and it shouldn't ever happen, but unfortunately it does.

This worst-case scenario is not the only way in which some financial advisors can devastate people. For instance, less scrupulous financial advisors probably will never tell you that they are only part-time advisors who don't keep abreast of information as diligently as other advisors do, or that they are only one signing away from making quota for the month, or that they are behind in their accreditation. There's a lot more that some advisors won't tell you, including whether they are criminal, negligent, or just plain incompetent, so it is up to you to know how to sniff these traits out so you can be confident when you hire one of the many good financial advisors available that he or she will assist *you* in managing your financial life.

Clearly (in hindsight), John's advisor was bogus because he turned out to be an outright criminal who was stealing money under the pretense of managing his clients' hard-earned savings. But what about advisors who sell you high-fee funds or insurance policies, so they can make more money, when there are better funds and policies on the market with lower fees? Assuming they have legitimate licenses, it wouldn't be fair to say that they're "bogus" advisors, but they are still a threat to your financial security, to a lesser degree, in that they are operating with some degree of conflict of interest, which can lead to bogus advice.

Or what about the advisor who isn't fully up to speed on the intricacies of tax consequences and gives you tax advice that is plain wrong? Or the advisor who sells you a mutual fund prior to a capital-gain distribution causing you to incur taxes on appreciation you did not participate in? Again, neither of these advisors is guilty of criminal action, but both are clearly inexperienced, unknowledgeable, or just plain incompetent. Such advisors can cause you major headaches (and heartache) and would be considered downright negligent compared to the astute planners out there.

We get calls on our helpline all the time from people who are looking for second opinions, wanting to know if their advisor is on the "up and up." The answer is usually yes, at least on the surface, because the vast majority of advisors are legitimate advisors who follow all the rules and regulations associated with selling financial securities and are disgusted by the thought of stealing their clients' money. However, just being ethical doesn't mean their advice is flawless. For any number of reasons, financial advisors may recommend investments that are overly expensive, overly risky, or simply inappropriate for their clients' financial situations and goals. Or they may inadvertently leave their clients less financially secure because they ignore key areas of financial planning simply because they aren't licensed to sell specific products and services. Some financial advisors may also have more clients than they can handle and so make critical mistakes with their accounts or find it difficult to stay as up-to-date as they should be on the latest tax and financial planning regulations.

Your challenge with any money you invest is to avoid both bogus advisors and bogus advice from advisors who just aren't at the top of their game for one reason or another. And the purpose of this chapter is to help you do that. Since bogus advisors—by which I mean those who are downright criminal—are easier to spot than their conflicted, unreliable, or incompetent counterparts and are much more dangerous and likely to threaten your entire nest egg, we turn to them first in order to learn how to beat them at their own game.

## THE BOGUS CRIMINAL ADVISOR:
## HOW TO KNOW IF YOU'RE DEALING WITH A "MADOFF"

When people call our helpline looking for a second opinion on an advisor they are considering, the bad apples we tell them about fall into two categories—those who are definitely bogus and those who are under suspicion of criminal behavior. We recommend that you stay away from both. The old saying "where there's smoke there's fire" definitely applies here.

In almost any story about someone who lost all his or her wealth by hiring a bogus advisor, there were red flags that can be identified in retrospect. When the advisor is getting what appear to be high returns in a tough market, it's easy to rationalize away the red flags because you want to believe this person can make you wealthy. It's such a compelling thought—that you found this brilliant person who can predict what the market is going to do and grow your money in a way that no one else can.

That's why Bernie Madoff's fund became "exclusive"—by invite only. It was a privilege to be "selected" as one of his investors because entire communities of people truly believed he knew something the rest of the financial services industry did not. They thought he had cracked the code—figured out the system—through his "top-secret" investment strategy, which he refused to reveal.

On paper, Madoff looked great—he had the right pedigree and even had close ties to the SEC. His track record was decades long, which is highly unusual for fraudulent advisors. He did run a legitimate trading business in addition to his fraudulent investment management busi-

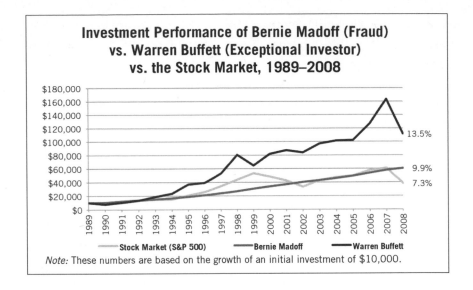

**Investment Performance of Bernie Madoff (Fraud) vs. Warren Buffett (Exceptional Investor) vs. the Stock Market, 1989–2008**

13.5%

9.9%

7.3%

Stock Market (S&P 500) — Bernie Madoff — Warren Buffett

*Note:* These numbers are based on the growth of an initial investment of $10,000.

ness. It's easy to see how many people, including very sophisticated managers of pension funds and foundations, believed he was the real deal. But even Bernie Madoff was putting out the kind of red flags that we see far too often when people call the financial helpline to get our opinion on what turns out to be a bogus advisor.

**Madoff's returns were both consistent and high, regardless of market conditions.** This is virtually impossible to achieve. Even Warren Buffett, who is widely lauded as the most successful investor of all time, has ups and downs, especially quarter to quarter and year to year, owing to economic conditions or other circumstances outside of his control. Over the period Madoff ran his scheme, Buffett provided his investors in Berkshire Hathaway (BRK.A) with a 14 percent average annualized return versus 7 percent for the stock market in general. However, for four of those 19 years (more than 20 percent of the time!), Buffett either lost money or underperformed the stock market because of circumstances he didn't foresee. Why? Because he is neither perfect nor psychic!

Madoff, on the other hand, didn't lose money in *any* of the 19 years he managed assets, despite peaks and valleys in the stock market and several economic upturns and downturns. His returns were always positive and rose steadily, regardless of economic conditions. This type of return is virtually impossible to achieve and is a huge red flag.

At best, any advisor who has generated consistently high returns quarter after quarter, despite economic conditions, is very lucky. If that's the case, you can't count on that luck to continue. In fact, most funds that have recently performed very well are likely to be overvalued and due for a correction. At worst—and mathematical probability makes this the more likely scenario—an advisor who generates near-"miraculous" returns for his or her clients is a fraud and those returns are simply the result of a Ponzi scheme whereby investors who request distributions are paid from other investors' money. This works until someone figures it out and alerts the authorities, or until too many investors request a distribution and there's not enough money to fulfill all the requests.

**Madoff generated his own financial statements rather than sending statements from his broker of record.** Generating his own statements was a huge red flag. Any financial statements you receive should come from the advisor's broker of record, who is responsible for tracking all the purchases and sales of securities in your account. These brokers are typically very large financial institutions, like Merrill Lynch, Bank of America, and Charles Schwab. Be wary of statements from any firm you've never heard of, and be especially wary of statements generated by your financial advisor or your advisor's firm.

**Madoff's trademark was to refuse to share his investment philosophy.** He argued that to do so would ruin his "edge," because other investors would copy what he was doing and drive up the prices of the investments he wanted to purchase. Even though this may sound like a legitimate concern, in reality it's not. All retail mutual funds are legally required to articulate their investment strategy and share that strategy with investors. Most private investment partnerships, or hedge funds, are expected to do the same to get assets from foundations, pension funds, or individuals with very high net worth.

There are really no "secrets" to investing that haven't already been revealed. In addition, investment strategies are only as good as their execution. You can have two portfolio managers who pursue the exact same strategy but come to dramatically different conclusions as to which investments will best fit that strategy and who then end up with significantly different results. Madoff knew this. The problem was that most of his individual investors didn't, and his institutional investors (pension funds and charitable foundations) exempted him from sharing his strategy because of his pedigree and long track record of consistently high returns.

Never invest with any financial advisor or investment manager who won't share his or her investment strategy. It is absolutely imperative not only that you know the investment strategy, but that you know it on a level on which you can discuss it intelligently with a good friend and answer his or her questions about it. You also should be totally comfortable that the investment strategy is a fit for your personal goals and level of risk tolerance, and you should verify that the investment advisor is following your investment strategy.

If together you and your advisor decided to invest 20 percent of your portfolio in large-cap value funds, then you need to make sure that the investments listed on your statements reflect this strategy. In this case, your statement should be filled with companies that you know, that typically have been in business for several decades, and that are in well-established, stable, and relatively safe industries. If you see a bunch of hot new social media companies on your statement, your advisor is *not* following the strategy you agreed upon and should be fired.

**Madoff wasn't a financial advisor in the true sense of the word.** He was a money manager. This discrepancy doesn't in and of itself make him bad—there are plenty of wonderful money managers who charge reasonable fees and do an excellent job managing money in line with their investment strategy. The problem occurs when people confuse a money manager with a financial advisor. A money manager invests money in one fund, while financial advisors develop custom plans based on individual needs and goals.

I was a money manager when I ran a hedge fund. We sold our hedge fund to our investors as part of their overall portfolio, but we didn't develop custom financial plans for them. Everyone was funneled into the same fund or managed accounts with the same investment strategy, and we did our best to beat other funds that were following the same strategy. The onus was on our investors to diversify their portfolios between our funds and other funds and investment opportunities, like real estate and venture capital or private equity (investing in well-established companies that need money to grow). Diversifying an investor's portfolio is the job of a financial advisor, and a good one will do this.

Far too many individual investors who turned over all their assets to Madoff viewed him as a financial advisor, thinking he was taking care of them financially on a more personal level than he would in fact have done even if he had been legitimate. Most of them would never have invested *all* their money in a typical mutual fund, like Fidelity Magellan Fund or PIMCO Total Return Fund—they wouldn't have wanted to put all their eggs in one basket. And I'm certain that most of Madoff's clients had well-diversified 401(k) accounts *before* they retired or liquidated the money they gave to Madoff.

Because Bernie Madoff was not a faceless mutual fund but a person whom many of his clients had met or knew well, the lines got blurred and thousands of them simply overlooked the need to diversify. Even though he was really a money manager, Madoff seemed like a financial advisor to his clients because he was their "guy." So instead of hiring a financial planner to create a diversified portfolio of investments designed to maximize their chances of meeting their specific financial goals, they did the opposite and invested everything in one bogus fund, managed by a bogus money manager who was running the world's biggest Ponzi scheme.

You can avoid the Bernie Madoffs of the world by doing two things:

## HOW I COST MY CLIENTS MILLIONS OF DOLLARS WITHOUT EVEN REALIZING IT: CONFESSIONS OF A RETIRED FINANCIAL PLANNER

"I worked in the financial services industry, selling investments and insurance, for 18 years. I was one of the good guys; my clients were family, friends, and friends of friends whom I cared about and socialized with. I felt a responsibility to do right by them, but also had to make my sales quotas, which wasn't always easy since I wasn't skilled at meeting new people and had to rely exclusively on my network. My firm was one of the better ones, but there were always fights over money (for example, how two advisors would split commissions on a sale they closed together), and there was a constant pressure to 'meet the numbers.'

"I was trained to sell investments that generated higher fees—like permanent life insurance and the firm's mutual funds, which carried a hefty front-end sales charge. I was also trained to regularly buy and sell mutual funds in an effort to make more money for the firm.

"What I tell you now is what I realized after the fact—everything was framed as an important step of the financial planning process. Sure, we needed to 'meet our numbers,' but the good news was that we were doing so in pursuit of a noble cause—helping our clients become financially secure and independent. We were told that we could 'do well' and 'do good.' Our clients *needed* our recommendations, and they needed to buy and sell investments regularly in order to ensure they had the best possible portfolio at any point in time. The actual training justified all the high-fee investments. Our firm, after all, was uniquely suited to investment and insurance planning, and our investors were paying for our expertise.

"The problem is that for people who really just want insurance coverage for a set period of time, the permanent life policies I sold were very expensive and, quite frankly, a waste of money. I know that now, but at the time we were all trained using a system that almost always favored permanent insurance over term insurance, and our firm's mutual funds over those offered by other firms. The training was highly compelling and was presented to us as financial planning training. I was 22, fresh out of college, when I started, so I had nothing to compare this with. I even ended up training hundreds of other planners on the financial planning system, thinking I was helping them and, ultimately, their clients.

"It wasn't until I was hired by an advisor who was telling people to refinance their homes in order to buy high-priced insurance policies that I realized that the industry had major problems. I was disgusted at his practices and his utter disregard for his clients, and I began to look back at my own training and sales practices in an effort to validate the profession I had chosen.

"What I learned was chilling. I realized I wasn't one of the good guys after all. All those years, I was really a financial services salesperson promoting specific financial products and services, not a financial planner in the true sense of the word. I educated myself on the principles of financial planning endorsed by the CERTIFIED FINANCIAL PLANNER™ Board of Standards and, with a pit lodged in my stomach, quit my job. Granted, I didn't rip any of my clients off, and their insurance and investments did increase in value and were a better alternative to them spending the money, *but* I could have saved many of them tens of thousands—in some cases, hundreds of thousands—of dollars simply by recommending lower-fee insurance policies and investments better suited to their needs.

"I left the industry to become a teacher, realizing that I wanted to be paid to help people, not to sell to them, and I haven't looked back since."

**1.** Hire a financial advisor with a fiduciary responsibility to act in your best interest, such as a CERTIFIED FINANCIAL PLANNER™ (CFP®) professional who can work with you to create a diversified portfolio of well-known mutual funds from established mutual fund companies that is designed around your specific needs.

**2.** Never give your advisor "discretion" over the management of your money. In other words, you should sign off on all investments the advisor makes on your behalf.

These two tasks may sound like a pain, but there are ways to mitigate the time and energy you spend on them and they are critical. Just as a smart business owner would not allow his or her CFO or accountant to write an unlimited number of checks without any sort of approval process, you should never allow an advisor to have *full* discretion over your assets. There is no balance in this scenario, and even the best advisors can stray into dangerous areas without proper oversight.

## FROM RED FLAG TO FLARE GUN:
## THE #1 THING A CRIMINAL WILL TELL YOU

In addition to the major red flags, there is one dead giveaway when it comes to spotting a bogus advisor. He or she *guarantees* a high return—usually a set percentage—with *no* risk. As much as we all might wish otherwise, this type of investment simply does not exist.

Deep down we all know that if it sounds too good to be true, it probably is. But it's easy to want to believe a very confident advisor who promises to make us wealthy beyond our wildest dreams. My best advice is to change "If it sounds too good to be true, it probably is," to "If it sounds too good to be true, it is absolutely, positively, a scam." No exceptions. Anyone who makes grandiose promises like this should be reported to the Financial Industry Regulatory Authority (FINRA) immediately. Simply by reporting such fraudulent claims before they get out of control, you may save thousands of people from losing everything.

## WHAT YOUR FINANCIAL ADVISOR ISN'T TELLING YOU

Here's the reality. There are fundamental conflicts of interest in the financial services industry that can hinder even the most well-intentioned advisors, and you need to be aware of these when you hire an advisor.

As with every major commitment you make in life, you need to understand what you are getting into before you sign on the dotted line. The same way someone is not going to willingly air all his or her dirty laundry on a first date, or your doctor is not going to disclose all the mistakes he or she has made treating patients, your financial advisor is not going to tell you anything that will scare you away—even if it is true.

What follows is what you won't hear but need to know when you interview financial advisors to find the right one:

> 1. "Generally, the higher the fee on the investment I sell you, the higher the commission I make in the end. This could cost you tens of thousands, or hundreds of thousands, of dollars over time."

**What this means:** Most advisors are paid commissions on the financial products and services they sell, and these vary by the type of product or service, among many other variables. The problem is that this system incentivizes advisors to sell high-fee investments, annuities, and insurance. This wouldn't be a bad thing if the financial markets were like real estate, where larger and nicer homes in better locations command higher prices (in other words, you get what you pay for). The problem is that high-fee mutual funds, annuities, and insurance policies typically perform worse than lower-fee options because the fees eat into your return. Takeaway: high fees significantly affect your ability to grow your wealth over time.

**How to protect yourself:** Make sure all the fees for the funds that your advisor recommends are at or below the industry average, using the chart on pages 64–65 as a guide. If you plan to invest for a very long time horizon, you may want to consider index funds, which can cost as little as under 0.2 percent of what you invest and typically outperform all other fund types.

A lot of the people we talk to don't even realize they're paying fees for their mutual funds. Many others think that the one-time commission they pay to their advisor and the small administrative fee they see on their statements are the only fees. But in the long run, both of these expenses are minuscule compared with the mutual fund's "expense ratio," which is the fee that the fund charges every year.

You can find the expense ratio in the fund's prospectus (that long document with lots of fine print that you got when you first purchased the fund but probably didn't have time to read), and usually it also can be found on the fund's website. It will look something like this: "1.12." No, that doesn't mean $1.12. It means 1.12 percent of the money you have invested in the fund—so for every $100,000 you have in there, you'll pay $1,120 *every single year.* You can see how that would really add up over time, and most people don't even know they're paying it.

### Fees for Selected Investment Objectives as an Annual Percentage of the Total Amount Invested

| Investment Objective | 10th Percentile | Median | 90th Percentile | Asset-Weighted Average | Simple Average |
|---|---|---|---|---|---|
| Equity funds[1] | 0.72% | 1.25% | 2.08% | 0.70% | 1.33% |
| Growth | 0.74% | 1.20% | 2.00% | 0.82% | 1.28% |
| Sector | 0.79% | 1.35% | 2.16% | 0.81% | 1.41% |
| Value | 0.73% | 1.18% | 1.96% | 0.80% | 1.25% |
| Blend | 0.45% | 1.08% | 1.89% | 0.46% | 1.12% |
| World | 0.88% | 1.39% | 2.20% | 0.86% | 1.46% |
| Hybrid funds[1] | 0.70% | 1.24% | 2.05% | 0.78% | 1.33% |
| Bond funds[1] | 0.48% | 0.86% | 1.65% | 0.57% | 0.98% |
| Taxable | 0.47% | 0.90% | 1.72% | 0.57% | 0.99% |

## Fees for Selected Investment Objectives
## as an Annual Percentage of the Total Amount Invested

| Investment Objective | 10th Percentile | Median | 90th Percentile | Asset-Weighted Average | Simple Average |
|---|---|---|---|---|---|
| Municipal | 0.50% | 0.80% | 1.57% | 0.56% | 0.93% |
| Money market funds[1] | 0.06% | 0.10% | 0.21% | 0.13% | 0.12% |
| Target date funds[2] | 0.49% | 0.94% | 1.61% | 0.57% | 0.99% |

*Sources:* Investment Company Institute and Lipper.
1. Data exclude mutual funds available as investment choices in variable annuities and mutual funds that invest primarily in other mutual funds.
2. Data include mutual funds that invest primarily in other mutual funds, but exclude mutual funds available as investment choices in variable annuities. Ninety-seven percent of these funds invest primarily in other mutual funds.

2. "I want to be your only financial advisor so I can make more money, even though I'm not qualified in some of the areas of financial planning that you need help with."

**What this means:** This may not sound like a big problem, but it becomes one when advisors take on more than they can handle because they don't want to take the risk of referring clients to another advisor who is an expert in areas they know little or nothing about. The result is that they overextend themselves and end up giving clients bad advice. Often a client would be better off being referred to a CPA, an estate planning attorney, or another professional who specializes in the area that is not the advisor's area of expertise.

**How to protect yourself:** Ask advisors about their experience and certifications and then verify this information. If they lack experience or certifications in a specific area—say taxes or insurance—you may want to consider adding another advisor to your "team" who specializes in that area. It is not at all uncommon for people to have a financial advisor who manages their portfolios and protects their assets with insurance and annuities, a CPA who helps them with tax planning—often coordinating with the financial advisor to create tax-efficient investment strategies—and an estate planning attorney who drafts the wills, trusts, and other legal documents needed to ensure that they have a solid plan to pass their assets on to their heirs.

> 3. "I'm trained to try to upsell you, because the more financial services you buy from me, the more money I make."

**What this means:** The pressure to "upsell" you causes advisors to sell you financial products and services you do not need. It is the reason people get overinsured and the reason so many people do things that may cost them dearly in the long run—like taking money out of their 401(k) or stopping new contributions in order to redirect money to their advisor, or refinancing their houses to invest more money with their advisor, or even paying the minimum on their high-interest-rate credit card debt to free up money to invest with their advisor.

**How to protect yourself:** Get a second and unbiased opinion. If your company is one of the many that are now offering unbiased financial education as a free employee benefit, you can talk to a financial planner who has no financial products or services to sell you and get an objective opinion on what your advisor is recommending. You can also turn to trusted sources on the Internet—like *Forbes* magazine (forbes.com), the Consumer Financial Protection Bureau (cfpb.org), the CERTIFIED FINANCIAL PLANNER™ Board of Standards (letsmakeaplan.org), and marketwatch.com. These sources will probably have information on the financial product or service your advisor is recommending, along with guidance on when it is appropriate and when it is a waste of your money. There are also fee-only planners who will charge you an hourly fee to review your financial plan and point out potential problems.

4. "My recommendations with respect to financial products and services are limited to the investments offered by the financial institution that employs me."

**What this means:** Even if there are clearly better investment options out there, this financial advisor is prohibited from selling them to you.

**How to protect yourself:** Ask prospective advisors if they are able to sell investments outside of what their employer offers. If the answer is no, chances are that you should decide not to limit your financial success by working with these advisors. If the answer is yes, find out exactly how selling outside investments affects each advisor. Do they get a significantly lower commission for selling outside investments, or do they get in trouble if they don't meet their quotas for selling the firm's proprietary investments? If either is the case, it's generally better to work with an advisor who has more flexibility—often an independent financial advisor who is not a financial salesperson for a large financial institution.

5. "I want you to buy and sell investments frequently, so I can make more money in fees and commissions."

**What this means:** The problem here is that the more often you buy and sell stocks, the more you may pay in fees and taxes, which can significantly drag down your return.

**How to protect yourself:** Do not give your financial advisor discretion to buy and sell investments on your behalf. Make sure that all financial transactions require your approval. Also, let your advisor know that you want to buy and hold your investments and sell only for three reasons:

**1.** *Your investment goals have changed or a material change to the mutual fund or investment makes it less attractive.* For example, a new portfolio manager may have taken over the mutual fund and changed the investment strategy in a way that makes you uncomfortable.

2. *Your portfolio has gotten out of balance.* Let's say you intentionally wanted to invest half your money in equity mutual funds that invest only in stocks and half your money in fixed-income mutual funds that invest only in bonds. Your intent was to hedge your bets a bit and diversify so that if stocks dropped significantly, your bonds would help offset your loss. Or vice versa. The market changes constantly, however, and over the course of a quarter or a year your equity mutual funds invested in stocks may go up or down by 10 to 20 percent, throwing off your original plan. In this case, it's wise to do what planners call "rebalancing" so that you can get back to your original plan—in this case, 50 percent in stocks, 50 percent in bonds.

3. *You're harvesting tax losses.* If you have an investment in a taxable account and it declines in value, you can sell it and use the loss to offset other taxes as long as you don't repurchase the same investment within 30 days.

6. "You are a small client to me, so I won't be giving you much time or attention. In fact, this is actually the last time you'll see or talk to me. One of my junior associates will take it from here."

**What this means:** Often a few legitimate advisors become very well known in a community, perhaps because they have a media presence on local news or radio, or because they have published a best-selling book on financial planning. They attract huge amounts of money and end up focusing their time and energy on people who have millions to invest. If your account is small by comparison, they often won't give you the time or care you need because they are already spread thin advising clients who have more money and can generate more in fees and commissions. You may walk out of the meeting thinking you are privileged to be working with "the best of the best," but in reality you'll most likely be delegated to an assistant advisor . . . or worse, no one at all.

Your account will then languish, without proper oversight. You may end up with a portfolio that is completely out of line with your goals and ill suited to provide distributions when you need the money—unless you take a significant loss. Or you may have undergone several critical life changes since you last met with your advisor, and these may have implications for how you should be investing or protecting your wealth. Without proper oversight, these changes get missed or never communicated to the advisor, and you end up with a financial plan that is completely wrong for you.

**How to protect yourself:** Look for an advisor whose clients are similar to you in terms of the amount of money they have to invest and their needs. Better to be a big (or at least medium-sized) fish in a small pond than a small fish in a big one. Ask advisors you interview how many clients they personally manage, how often they meet with these clients, and how they manage their client base so that everyone gets the personal attention they need. If you don't get a very strong answer to this question, cross those advisors off your list and move on.

7. "I have very little experience in financial planning and am just learning the ropes."

**What this means:** Remember Tamara from the introduction who chose to invest her money with her friend? He was moonlighting as a financial advisor, and he made two big mistakes. First, he took on too much risk and she experienced a significant loss. Then he sold the investments for a loss and put her in GM bonds without doing any research on the quality of those bonds, and she lost almost everything as a result. The friend was a great guy and not technically a bogus advisor—he had his licenses to sell securities, didn't hold himself out as having designations or experience he didn't have, and didn't commit fraud. But he still managed to lose all her money through massive incompetence. Financial planning requires proper training. Like a surgeon who is not properly trained and is prone to make mistakes, your financial advisor may simply not have the training, knowledge, or experience to deliver sound advice to you.

**How to protect yourself:** Look for advisors with at least 10 years of experience in financial planning, and ask them what designations they have. The next section goes into more detail on designations. While no designation guarantees that an advisor is current on key areas of financial planning, designations do offer a layer of protection. All strong designations require extensive education, testing, and continued education, so advisors who have them are much more likely to have the knowledge and experience required to provide you with sound financial advice.

## IMPLEMENT A VERIFICATION PROCESS—NO MATTER WHAT

Now that we know who you *don't* want to work with, let's turn to what you should be looking for when verifying that your advisor is who he says he is. The good news is that it's very easy to do background checks on advisors to validate that they have the experience, expertise, and legal clearances that they say they have. What's the bad news? That's only the beginning of your responsibilities for verifying your advisor.

### Financial Designations

First ask an advisor for a list of his or her designations and licenses. Financial designations are harder to earn than licenses, and they typically require significant education as well as testing to validate knowledge, as well as continuing education to ensure that an advisor stays current. Licenses legally enable advisors to sell securities and investments, which is necessary if they are selling you investments or managing your money instead of simply making recommendations for a fee. In the majority of cases, you will look to your advisor to conduct financial transactions, so it is important to know that person is legally allowed to do so as a minimum requirement. Keep in mind, however, that legal clearance to sell securities is like a driver's license: it means you passed a test but in no way guarantees you are a good driver.

Designations, on the other hand, are equivalent to becoming a professional race-car driver. Like race-car drivers (certainly all the good ones), financial advisors must undergo significant training and testing, and it's not easy—the pass rate for the exam to become a CERTIFIED FINANCIAL PLANNER™ (CFP®) certificant, for example, is about the same as the pass rate on the bar exam that law school grads are required to take in order to practice law.

Listed in the following chart are the important credentials for financial advisors, along with the website you can use to verify that the financial advisor you are considering possesses these credentials and is in good standing—meaning that there are no complaints or disciplinary actions on his or her record. We recommend, at minimum, that you find an advisor with a CFP® designation, as this is considered the gold standard for financial planning and shows that this person has truly committed to the field and exhibited the discipline to complete the education and the knowledge to pass the testing—which is completed by only a small minority of "financial advisors." But also be aware of other designations that signify high quality and may be particularly important for your situation.

| Designation | What the Designation Covers | Training Requirements | When It's Important That Your Advisor Have This Designation | How to Verify That Your Advisor Has This Designation |
|---|---|---|---|---|
| CERTIFIED FINANCIAL PLANNER™ (CFP®) | All major areas of financial planning | Bachelor's degree and financial planning course work; three years of experience or two years of apprenticeship; exam | You want a comprehensive financial plan to meet your goals, along with someone who will implement and adjust them with your approval. | Contact the CFP® Board: cfp.net. |

| Designation | What the Designation Covers | Training Requirements | When It's Important That Your Advisor Have This Designation | How to Verify That Your Advisor Has This Designation |
|---|---|---|---|---|
| Certified Public Accountant and Personal Financial Specialist (CPA/PFS) | Accounting (CPA) plus financial planning (PFS) | For CPAs, bachelor's degree with accounting course requirements, one or more years of experience, and exam; for PFSs, financial planning education and two years of experience | You have advanced tax planning needs owing to high income and/or a complex financial situation. | Contact the American Institute of CPAs: aicpa.org. |
| Chartered Financial Consultant (ChFC) | Similar curriculum to CFP® plus additional advanced financial planning course work | Similar to CFP® plus insurance course work and three years of experience | You are looking for comprehensive financial planning for specialized objectives, including special needs planning, business succession planning, and wealth transfer. Many ChFC holders also hold the CFP® designation. | Contact DesignationCheck: designationcheck.com. |
| Chartered Life Underwriter (CLU) | Financial planning with a focus on insurance | Course work; three years of experience | You have complex issues related to life insurance and estate and tax planning, such as multigenerational wealth transfer, a blended family, or a closely held business. | Contact DesignationCheck: designationcheck.com. |

| Designation | What the Designation Covers | Training Requirements | When It's Important That Your Advisor Have This Designation | How to Verify That Your Advisor Has This Designation |
|---|---|---|---|---|
| Certified Investment Management Analyst (CIMA) | Investing | Education program; exam | You're looking for someone to choose and monitor your investment managers. | Contact the Investment Management Consultants Association: imca.org. |
| Chartered Financial Analyst (CFA) | Financial analysis, advanced portfolio management, economics, and corporate finance | Bachelor's degree; four years of experience; exam | You need advanced investment management, especially with individual securities. | Contact the CFA Institute: cfainstitute.org. |

## Licenses

Next, check on the licenses possessed by your potential financial advisor. The best way to do this is through the website of the Financial Industry Regulatory Authority (finra.org), which tracks every single advisor who is legally permitted to sell securities. Enter your advisor's name into the FINRA database and you'll learn what securities licenses this person actually has and, even more important, whether or not any complaints, disciplinary actions, suspensions, or very frequent changes of employment appear on his or her record. Registered Investment Advisors (RIA) or Registered Investment Advisor Representatives are regulated by the SEC and can be verified and researched at adviserinfo.sec.gov /IAPD/Content/IapdMain/iapd_SiteMap.aspx. The SEC also has a web page, Protect Your Money, with links to FINRA, RIA information, and state securities regulators: sec.gov/investor/brokers.htm.

You'll want to see a completely clean record, with validation that the advisor is current and in good standing with all the licenses he or she possesses to sell securities. Even a single complaint, and certainly any disciplinary action, is a major red flag. When it comes to your money, it's simply safer and more prudent not to give your advisor the benefit of the doubt if his or her FINRA record is troubling. FINRA reviews all complaints, and while I have known advisors who have had an illegitimate complaint on their record, most complaints tend to be legitimate. Be especially cautious if there are multiple complaints, or if the complaint is very serious in nature.

Beyond complaints, disciplinary actions or suspensions are a whole other story. If you see any of these—run! Under no circumstances do you ever want to invest money with an advisor who has gotten in trouble with the law. There are simply too many good, legitimate advisors out there with clean track records to take this kind of risk with your money.

## ADDITIONAL STEPS YOU CAN TAKE TO PROTECT YOURSELF

Strong designations and a clean record are important, but they do not guarantee that your advisor is looking out for your best interest. After checking on designations and licenses, we recommend that you take the following steps to further validate that your advisor has the integrity, knowledge, and experience to provide you with the best possible advice.

**1. Find out if your advisor is willing to take "fiduciary responsibility" for the advice he or she gives you and willing to document this in all agreements you sign.** A fiduciary is legally required to act in your best interest and can be sued for taking actions that are not in line with your best interest—like overcharging you by selling overly expensive or unnecessary investments; not taking proper care to align your portfolio with your goals and to make adjustments to your financial plan as needed; not disclosing the risks of investments; or incurring costly mistakes by misrepresenting his or her level of knowledge and expertise about key aspects of financial planning. Very few financial advisors hold themselves out to be fiduciaries, and even fewer will sign an agreement that states, in no uncertain terms, that they are operating in a fiduciary capacity as your advisor. However, if you can find one who is willing to do this, you are automatically putting yourself in a safer position.

**2. Make sure you know exactly how the advisor is compensated for each investment he or she recommends and the impact of those fees on your overall return.** Some advisors are compensated by commission, while others are compensated for having assets under management. "Fee-based" advisors may charge asset-based fees but either they or their firms are not restricted from receiving additional income from certain commissions or distribution fees. "Fee-only" advisors, as defined by the National Association of Personal Financial Advisors (NAPFA), are those that are compensated solely by the client with neither the advisor nor any related party receiving any compensation that is contingent on the purchase or sale of any financial product. While most fee-only advisors charge asset-based management fees, a growing number of advisors work on an hourly fee or annual retainer. The compensation structure that is best for you may depend on the level of service you require from the advisor. For example, someone who is looking for one-time investment advice may benefit from the commission structure, while someone who is looking for ongoing asset management may prefer an asset-based model. Many people find working with a fee-only advisor who charges by the hour or per project to be the lowest-cost and most unbiased solution.

**3. Look for signs of honesty.** Look for advisors who share both the pros and the cons of investments, who are up-front about what they can and cannot do and about what they do and do not know, and who are willing to refer you to other financial professionals for help with taxes, estate planning, etc.

# 4

## Avoiding the Worst Investments:
## The Best-Performing Mutual Funds

**How often have** you heard of a money manager who just had his or her worst quarter or year being asked for their investment recommendations? By and large, that track record doesn't go over well in a television segment on investing:

> *"Here's John Smith, who lost a whole lot of money on the investments he made last year for his clients . . . Let's find out what he thinks we should invest in!"*

How often has your advisor touted the low returns of a particular mutual fund before recommending that you invest in that very fund? I would wager not very often!

What if I could prove to you that investments that did poorly over a given quarter or year are more likely to do well the next quarter or year than investments that just did exceptionally well?

How does it feel when I pose that question? If you are like most people, the very concept makes you uncomfortable. You wouldn't promote the worst-performing employee on your team. Why? Because his or her track record doesn't merit it. But now, suddenly, someone is suggesting that you *ignore* the track records of investments when your own money is at stake?

Your confusion is one reason the financial services industry continues to tout high-performing funds and actually discontinues funds that don't perform well in order to boost their "historical returns." Knowing that you are much more likely to put your money in a mutual fund that has done exceptionally well, the industry centers much of its marketing efforts on these funds.

Most financial advisors follow this lead. They don't want to be accused of selling their clients "loser" funds. It's a lot easier for an advisor to justify selling a fund that loses money if, say, *Money* magazine has published an article on it as the "hot fund of the year" because of its exceptional performance. But if a fund that has historically lost money loses more money *after* you invest in it, your advisor looks like, well, an idiot. And that's not good for business.

And so one of the biggest myths in the investment world continues—namely, that the best-performing mutual funds make the best long-term investments.

What your financial advisor isn't telling you is that the best-performing funds typically make the worst investments, and here's the data to prove it. Released twice per year, the S&P Persistence Scorecard tracks the continuity of top-performing mutual funds. Yearly consecutive periods are compared with the next period to measure "persistence." Referencing the December 2013 scorecard, Rick Ferri, managing partner and chief compliance officer of Portfolio Solutions®, wrote, "Funds that perform in the top half of their peer group during a five-year period had a less than 50 percent chance of staying in the top half during the next five-year period."* Investors have better odds choosing an investment out of a hat than using past performance to choose winners.

For example, there's a 25 percent chance that you would pick a fund

---

\* Rick Ferri, "Coin Flipping Outdoes Active Fund Managers," January 13, 2014, http://www.rickferri.com/blog/strategy/coin-flipping-outdoes-active-fund-managers.

that was in the top half of top performers over three consecutive 12-month periods. But the Persistence Scorecard for June 2014 found that among funds in the top half, only 14.1 percent of large-cap funds (companies with a market capitalization value of more than $10 billion), 16.32 percent of mid-cap funds (market capitalization value of $2 billion to $10 billion), and 25 percent of small-cap funds ($300 million to $2 billion) were able to do that.* That S&P Persistence Scorecard also showed "a likelihood" that the best-performing funds would become the worst-performing funds, "and vice versa."

What if you ignore short-term performance and look at longer-term performance? The study found that "an inverse relationship exists between the measurement time horizon and the ability of top-performing funds to maintain their status." In other words, the longer the time period, the less likely it is that a top-performing fund will continue outperforming in the future.

## THE 3 PERCENT RETURN ADVANTAGE

So if you shouldn't be investing in "hot" mutual funds (what we call "chasing returns"), how should you select your investments? Is there any way to maximize your chances of getting a good return while still containing your risk so that you don't lose a lot of money when the market goes down?

It turns out that there is, but it runs completely counter to the way most financial advisors make money, so most people have never even heard about it. We call it the "3 percent return advantage," because that's what it's designed to help you achieve over long periods of time — annual returns that, on average, are 3 percent higher per year than what

---

* Aye Soe, "Does Past Performance Matter? The Persistence Scorecard," S&P Dow Jones Indices, June 2014, http://www.spindices.com/documents/spiva/persistence-scorecard-june-2014.pdf.

most investors earn on their investments in a given year. Please note, however, that the two operative terms here are "designed" and "long periods of time."

*No one* can guarantee you will receive a 3 percent greater return in a given year by following any investment strategy. *No one* can guarantee you will receive that kind of return over time in 40 years. All that we can responsibly do is give you a formula that puts the odds in your favor. It doesn't mean you won't suffer painful losses or that friends who try to time the market—investing in the hottest stocks, bonds, and mutual funds—won't sometimes get lucky.

But as with any sport, the best you can do when you play the game is to set yourself up for success—do the right things based on proven principles, with as much consistency as possible, and you can dramatically increase your chances of winning. And that's precisely what the 3 percent return advantage does for you—it positions you to have the greatest probability of success. Here are the three steps involved that add up to the 3 percent return advantage. Once you see how it works, you'll understand why so few financial advisors advocate that you follow this strategy.

### Step 1: Invest in mutual funds with very low fees.
### (return advantage: 1.17 percent)

**Why this is a good idea:** With mutual funds, paying fees (called mutual fund expense ratios) is guaranteed. They are the only thing you know will happen for sure and the only thing you have any control over. You can deliberately invest in low-fee mutual funds, but you can't deliberately choose funds that are guaranteed to perform well over the next month, quarter, year, or decade. And unlike most things in life, you don't get what you pay for when it comes to investing in mutual funds.

The more you pay, the *less* you get. Forgive the following Gen X reference, but I like to think of fees as little Pac-Men that eat into my wealth. Yes, I have to pay something, but I make sure it's as little as possible.

The chart below shows how the cost of fees can affect investment returns over time, based on an investment of $50,000.

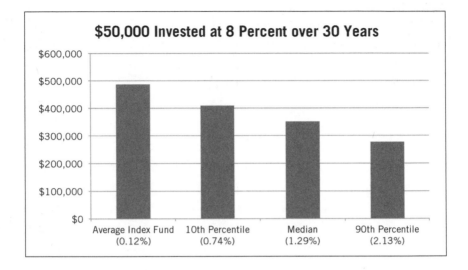

When we talk about the Standard & Poor's 500, we are talking about what is known as a stock index. Different stock indexes can track different segments of the stock market, including large, medium, or small companies, or the market as a whole. The S&P 500 is a popular stock index that is comprised of the largest 500 companies traded on the stock exchange—as measured by their total value (also called market capitalization). A mutual fund that invests in the securities of a particular index is called an "index fund." Index funds are designed to closely follow the performance of the underlying index. Index funds tend to have the lowest fees because instead of hiring expensive managers and research analysts to try to beat the market, as "actively" managed funds do, they simply "buy the market." As a result, their fees are much lower and their average longer-term performance is actually better than the vast majority of actively managed funds.

Intuitively, most investors gravitate toward actively managed funds because they want to "beat" the market, not simply "tie" it, which is what index funds essentially do. Actively managed funds play into our competitive instincts and our expectation that we should do "better than average." Simply accepting market returns, many people believe, is a form of giving up when, after all, actively managed funds have the *potential* to beat their market index. There's also a widespread belief that portfolio managers, who buy and sell the investments in a mutual fund, have some sort of edge and are highly qualified, based on their experience, to make strong investments that will outperform the market.

However, both academic theory (called the "Efficient Market Hypothesis") and empirical results show that this just isn't the case. It's *really* hard to beat the market, especially when you factor in the drag of fees on your returns. Perhaps that's why a recent Morningstar study found that "if there's anything in the whole world of mutual funds that you can take to the bank, it's that expense ratios help you make a better decision. In every single time period and data point tested, low-cost funds beat high-cost funds."* In fact, Morningstar found low fees to be the single best indicator of superior future performance—better even than its own star ratings!

Even Warren Buffett, widely considered the greatest investor alive today, has recommended that people invest in index funds. He has actually instructed his trustees to invest his assets in index funds for his wife when he passes away, saying, "I believe the trust's long-term results from this policy will be superior to those attained by most investors—whether pension funds, institutions, or individuals—who employ high-fee managers." (Buffett also made a $1 million bet for charity that an index fund would beat a group of top hedge funds over 10 years; with only three years left, the index fund is way ahead.†)

So why would so many mutual fund managers be making hundreds of thousands of dollars a year if they don't actually add significant value?

---

\* Russel Kinnel, "How Expense Ratios and Star Ratings Predict Success," Morningstar, August 9, 2010, http://news.morningstar.com/articlenet/article.aspx?id=347327.

† Alex Crippen, "Buffett Has Big Lead in Bet Against Hedge Funds," CNBC, February 6, 2014, http://www.cnbc.com/id/101394085.

I wish I had the answer. This is one of the most frustrating things we see as financial educators.

**What your financial advisor isn't telling you:** Most financial advisors get paid in one of two ways. They sell you mutual funds for a commission, or they charge you a fee to choose and manage a portfolio of funds for you. Either way, they tend to love showing you funds that have outperformed the general market because people are more likely to want to invest in funds with great track records.

Advisors also often justify their fees by their ability to select funds that outperform the market. What often happens, though, is that in any given year some of the funds they recommend will outperform and some won't. They then replace the underperforming funds with other funds that have outperformed. Next year, rinse and repeat.

If you knew that most of those outperforming funds won't continue to outperform and that you're probably better off with a simple portfolio of low-cost index funds, you might decide that you don't need to pay for the advisor's services. As we've seen and will continue to see throughout this book, there are lots of other ways in which a good advisor can add tremendous value, but predicting which funds will outperform the market isn't one of them.

### Step 2: Look for funds with low turnover.
### (meaning they buy and sell investments very infrequently, and instead hold most of their investments for a long period of time; return advantage: 1.3 percent)

**Why this is a good idea:** Mutual fund fees aren't the only cost of owning a mutual fund. Hidden costs known as "trading costs" are not disclosed to you because they aren't a fee that the mutual fund company is charging you. Instead, they add costs like brokerage commissions on trades, the difference between the bid and ask price on a stock, and the fact that a large fund can push the price of a stock higher when it buys it and lower the price when it sells it. All of this adds up to lower returns on your money.

How much lower? According to the *Wall Street Journal,* a recent study of thousands of US stock funds found that average trading costs add up to about 1.44 percent of assets, ranging from 0.14 percent in the bottom 25 percent and 2.96 percent in the top 25 percent. Here's how much those trading costs can affect $50,000 invested over 30 years with an otherwise 8 percent rate of return:

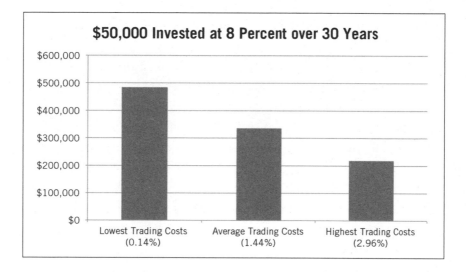

The results are even starker here: the funds with the highest trading costs earn less than half of what is earned by the ones with the lowest trading costs. So how do you find out what a fund's trading costs are? It's hard to find out directly, but you can look at the fund's turnover ratio, which is a measurement of how often the fund trades. The more often the fund trades, the higher its trading costs tend to be, so look for funds with a low turnover ratio, generally 25 percent or below.

Guess which funds tend to trade the least? *Index funds.* By not actively trading, they're able to keep trading costs lower and thus put more money in your pocket.

## Step 3: Rebalance your portfolio so that you buy low and sell high. (return advantage: 0.47 percent)

**Why this is a good idea:** "Rebalancing your portfolio" means sticking to the mix of stocks, bonds, and cash that you've decided is the best fit for your financial situation. When one part of your portfolio—say, bonds—becomes a much larger portion of your portfolio because the bond market is up and the stock market is down, you can readjust: buy stocks (or equity mutual funds) and sell bonds (or fixed-income mutual funds) to bring your portfolio back into balance and stay on course with your original investment strategy.

In addition to staying the course with your investment strategy, you are also doing something else that should benefit you over time—selling bonds *after* they have had a nice gain (selling high) and buying stocks after they have declined in value (buying low). Common sense tells us to buy low and sell high, but that's hard to do without rebalancing your portfolio at least once a year because we have no way of knowing when the market is going to peak and when it's going to stabilize. Rebalancing takes the guesswork—or human emotions—out of the equation by incorporating buying and selling into a process of keeping your portfolio on track. You should consider rebalancing at regular intervals, such as every three months, once a year, or when one asset class (stocks or bonds) grows to be 10 percent more than your original allocation. For example, instead of keeping a portfolio balance that has become 40 percent bonds and 60 percent stocks when 50/50 is the target allocation, selling some stocks and buying some bonds will allow bonds to return to 50 percent so that your allocation is back to the percentages you originally intended.

Because of the built-in tendency with portfolio rebalancing to buy low and sell high, many financial experts estimate that rebalancing can add up to 1 percent a year in higher returns. The results can vary widely, however, so let's be conservative and call it half a percent. For example, one study compared a portfolio that was rebalanced every quarter from

January 1, 1992, to May 31, 2012, with one that wasn't rebalanced and found that the rebalanced portfolio earned 0.47 percent more per year.*

**Red Flag Alert—When a financial advisor doesn't bring up the advantages of portfolio rebalancing:** A financial advisor who has your best interest at heart should *always* bring up rebalancing because they know how important it is to manage your risk and to set up a process where you are likely to buy low and sell high. So if your advisor isn't talking about the importance of rebalancing with you, or worse, is encouraging you to put more money into stocks or stock mutual funds (also called equity mutual funds) when the market is soaring or to sell when it plummets, this is a major red flag. It means that your advisor is enabling emotional investing rather than providing the balanced perspective you hired him or her to give you.

## The 3 Percent Return Advantage: Add It Up

When you add up the return advantages from these three steps—1.17 percent from investing in low-fee mutual funds, plus 1.3 percent from investing in mutual funds with low turnover, plus 0.47 percent from rebalancing your portfolio—the total is a return advantage of approximately 3 percent. What this means is that *by investing in funds with low fees and low turnover and rebalancing periodically, you can increase your returns by 3 percent per year compared with investing in funds with average fees and turnover and not rebalancing.*

Index funds, with their low fees and low turnover, capture most of the 3 percent return advantage outside of your retirement plan. You may have target date funds in your company's retirement plan that use a variety of different index funds and automatically rebalance them as

---

* Gregg S. Fisher, "The Value of Rebalancing," *Forbes,* June 22, 2012, http://www.forbes.com/sites/greggfisher/2012/06/22/the-value-of-rebalancing/.

needed. A target date fund could be the best option for you to get the 3 percent return advantage in your company's retirement plan.

Three percent may not sound like a whole lot, but let's see how that translates into real dollars over time. Here is that same $50,000 invested at 8 percent versus 5 percent over 30 years:

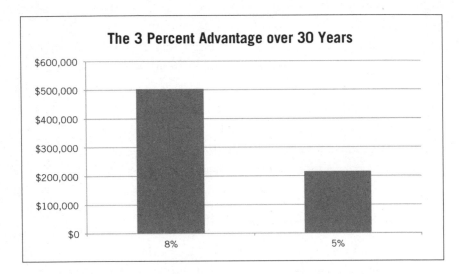

That 3 percent difference gives you about two and a half times as much money—which in this case is almost $300,000! Not bad for a strategy that doesn't require you to spend much time researching funds or following the market. All you have to do is look for low costs and take a few minutes rebalancing each year. Where else in life are you rewarded for being both cheap and lazy?

## SO DO YOU NEED AN ADVISOR TO HELP YOU INVEST?

Like most things in life, the answer to this question is: it depends.

First, before you hire a financial advisor, you should *max* out your retirement plan, health savings account, and other company benefits and also pay down your high-interest-rate debt. If you haven't done these things, not only is it too early to hire an advisor, but you will risk missing out on the chance to invest your money in ways that are likely to bring you a significantly higher return than any return an advisor could provide.

Let's say you follow this guidance and delay hiring a financial advisor until you max out your company benefits, but you are overwhelmed by the investment options for your 401(k) plan. You want professional advice on how to invest within your 401(k). In this case, there are some great solutions that don't require going to an advisor (who will typically focus on accounts *outside* your company benefits). Ask your benefits manager if your 401(k) has two options that are becoming increasingly common in retirement plans: "in-plan advice" and "target date funds." These options basically do all the work for you so that you don't need to actively select your investments (or even actively rebalance them).

Target date funds are mutual funds that fully diversify your investments based on your age or the year closest to when you want to retire. Setting up target date funds in no way guarantees that you will retire on time, but it does mean that the fund is using an investment strategy that puts together a portfolio of stocks, bonds, and cash tailored to your retirement time frame. You simply pick the target date fund that is closest to when you want to retire. For example, pick target date 2020 if you are close to retirement, target date 2035 if you are in midcareer, and target date 2055 if you just started working.

Target date funds are a very good option if you don't want to actively manage your account and if you don't have a lot of outside assets that have implications for how you invest the money in your 401(k) plan.

If you have a target date fund that's also made up of index funds, you're in luck! You not only get the advantage of diversification, but you also get the advantage of lower expenses. Just be aware that some target date funds may add fees on top of the underlying funds or use actively managed funds, which tend to be more expensive than index funds. Regardless, studies have shown that investors who utilize investment help through options like target date funds tend to outperform "do-it-yourself" investors who select and manage their own investments in their retirement plan. As such, the extra cost may be worth it for most people, especially if you are committed to following the principles outlined in the 3 percent return advantage laid out previously.

The managed account option in your retirement plan may be your best bet if you have a more complex financial situation. Let's say that (1) you're married and want to take into account how your spouse is investing in his or her 401(k), (2) you also have some company stock options that could be worth a lot but could also end up worthless depending on how successful your company becomes, and (3) you have a 529 plan invested very aggressively for your daughter's college education. A managed account option, which automatically manages the money in your 401(k) plan for you, can take all these factors into account.

Studies show that investors in managed accounts and target date funds generally do better (by three percentage points on average per year) than those who go it alone. But managed accounts are expensive, typically costing 0.15 to 0.7 percent depending on the size of your account and the size of your plan: the larger both are, the lower the fee tends to be. This fee is in addition to the fees you are paying on the funds in which your money is automatically invested, so you have to be sure your situation merits paying this fee.

So far, in all these scenarios, you don't need a financial advisor. In fact, a financial advisor could be detrimental to your wealth by taking your focus off paying off debts and investing in your company benefits.

It's time to consider an advisor, however, if you are a busy individual, you have no high-interest-rate debt, you have invested up to the maximum in your 401(k) and HSA, and you have significant disposable income that you'd like to invest. In this situation, an advisor *can* help you. A good advisor who is a true *financial planner* will take into account your entire financial situation and create an investment strategy that makes the most sense based on your circumstances and goals. This advisor may not generate strong returns every year, or even steady returns every year, but he or she will ensure that your investment strategy stays on track, that you invest in a tax-efficient manner, and that you don't respond emotionally to sudden changes in the market. In truth, much of what a good advisor does is save people from themselves. Left to our own devices, studies show that most of us end up neglecting our investments, making emotional decisions about our investments, or accidentally falling into tax traps that cost us far more than a planner's advice would have.

You may be an exception to this rule if you discover that you truly love investing, you can maintain a disciplined investment strategy, and you are willing to learn tax planning and to stay on top of current tax law. I love investing myself, and I know the basics of tax planning, but when it comes to my money I get emotional, so I use an advisor who keeps me on track. Most of the CERTIFIED FINANCIAL PLANNER™ professionals I employ also use an advisor, though a couple of them (who also happen to be the most disciplined with their diets and exercise) choose to forgo the fees and manage their money themselves.

## HOW TO CREATE A WINNING INVESTMENT STRATEGY WITHOUT THE HELP OF AN ADVISOR

If you either don't need an advisor or don't want one, there are options available to you (besides the in-plan advice I mentioned in the previous section) for maximizing your chances of success.

First, you have to know the basics, or else you are walking around, metaphorically speaking, with a loaded gun and no idea how or when to use it (and the gun is pointed at yourself).

What are those basics?

### 1. Investing Your Money Based on Different Goals

Investments are like vehicles that get you from where you are to where you want to be. So whenever you invest money, you should always start with your goal. You wouldn't take a plane to the supermarket, and you probably wouldn't want to bicycle from LA to NYC, so make sure you choose the proper investments as well.

*Short-Term Goals (Five Years or Less)*

You want to keep your money safe. That means putting cash into a bank account or money market fund that doesn't fluctuate in value. If you invest short-term money in something like stocks, you may find that it's down in value when you need it. You'll be forced to sell it at a loss or, even worse, you may no longer have enough money for your goal.

*Longer-Term Goals (More Than Five Years)*

For longer-term goals, you can afford to put your money into riskier investments like stocks and bonds, and the longer your time frame the riskier your overall portfolio can be. The advantage of riskier investments is that they tend to earn more in the long run, especially stocks. The downside is that they're, well, risky.

One way to reduce that risk is through diversification. They say don't put all your eggs in one basket, and that's especially true for individual stocks and corporate bonds. An individual stock or bond is extremely risky because it can go to zero (remember Enron?) and never recover. That's why no more than 10 to 15 percent of your portfolio should be in any one stock or bond, especially if it's your company. After all, you don't want to lose your job and your nest egg at the same time should something happen to your employer.

On the other hand, if you have many stocks and bonds that represent the entire US economy or even the world economy, it would take a global meltdown for them all to be worthless. In that case, your portfolio would be the least of your problems. (This is why some people further "diversify" into stockpiles of food, precious metals, and even guns and ammo.)

And while you can build a diversified portfolio of stocks and bonds on your own with enough knowledge, time, and money, it's a lot easier to do so with mutual funds. With a mutual fund, you're pooling your money with a lot of other investors in the fund and basically paying an investment firm (these are the fees we talked about earlier) to invest the money for you. Just try to stick to low-cost funds as much as possible.

## 2. Knowing Your Risk Tolerance

If you can't sleep well at night when your portfolio loses value, tempting you to bail out, you're probably a more conservative investor. If you see downturns as an opportunity to buy more on sale, you're probably more aggressive. If you're in between, you're probably a moderate investor.

Aggressive investors can tolerate having more money in more aggressive investments (like stocks) that tend to earn more but are also more volatile. Conservative investors invest more in less risky investments that are steadier but don't tend to earn as much (such as bonds). Moderate investors, as you might expect, are right in the middle.

### Risk Tolerance

|  | Conservative | Moderate | Aggressive |
|---|---|---|---|
| Stocks | 30–40% | 50–60% | 75–85% |
| Bonds | 40–60% | 30–40% | 10–20% |
| Cash | 0.50% | 10–20% | 5–15% |

If you're not sure how to diversify your money based on your risk tolerance, there are lots of different asset allocation models you can choose from. Your employer's retirement plan provider may provide some, or you can find some in various books or on websites. Above are some sample long-term portfolios for each type of investor.

## 3. Choosing Mutual Funds

Once you have decided how to diversify your portfolio, it's time to select the individual funds for each category or asset class. Check with your 401(k) provider or IRA custodian to see what funds are available in your retirement account. Do the same with your non-retirement accounts, including your HSA, 529 plan, and taxable brokerage account. Your options may include actively managed funds, index funds, and target date funds.

As we discussed earlier, index funds tend to offer better performance because they have lower fees and trading costs, so use them to build your portfolio. If index funds are not available, look for an actively managed fund with low fees and low turnover. Try not to let historical performance influence your decision. Although the financial services industry likes to promote past performance, as we have seen, you can't buy past performance. That ship has already sailed.

If you don't want to be actively involved in selecting the individual funds for each asset class, consider using a target date fund, if available. If you are a moderate investor, choose the target date fund closest to the date you plan to start withdrawing funds from your account. If you are aggressive, you can use a longer target date, and if you are conservative, you can use a shorter target date. As with most target date funds, you get the benefits of diversification, automatic rebalancing, and asset allocation gradually getting more conservative as you approach your target date.

## 4. Minimizing Your Taxes

Of course, investments are not just about what you earn, but about what you keep. Here are three steps you can take to minimize the tax bite on your investments:

**1.** Max out tax-sheltered accounts like 401(k) plans, IRAs, and 529 plans (for college savings) before investing in a taxable account.

**2.** If you have a mix of taxable and tax-sheltered accounts, put the investments that generate the most income into the tax-sheltered accounts first.

**3.** For taxable accounts, take advantage of losses by selling them so you can use the losses to offset profits you realized from other investments for the purposes of lowering your taxable investment income.

**4.** Consider gifting appreciated stock to charities and to minors instead of giving them cash.

**5.** If you're unsure about how to do any of the above, consider hiring a financial advisor who is savvy in tax-aware investing.

You can learn more about each of these steps in chapter 5 on taxes.

## HOW TO ENSURE THAT YOUR ADVISOR IS DOING A GOOD JOB INVESTING YOUR MONEY

At the end of the day, the most important takeaway from this book is that no one cares about your money more than you do. Even if you hire an expert financial advisor, it's still incumbent upon you to make sure that you select, manage, and evaluate your advisor, and doing so effectively requires having baseline knowledge about what's involved in doing a good job. Without that knowledge, you probably won't recognize if it's time to fire your advisor and hire a new one. And yes, people do fire their advisors if they feel they aren't getting their money's worth (pun intended).

This chapter started by bursting a commonly held myth and showing that the funds that are "hot" right now and issue higher short-term returns often make for the worst investments over the long term. When your money is invested this way, you can't simply look at your financial statement and determine whether your advisor "has your back" and is worth the fees you are paying him or her. Ironically, a really high return over a short period of time actually could be a red flag.

One of the best safeguards when you are working with an advisor is to let that person know that you want to follow the steps to set you up for the 3 percent return advantage outlined in this chapter. If he or she either refuses to do so or makes a commitment to follow these principles but doesn't honor it, then you'll want to find an advisor who will. Virtually all of the research done in the field of investing shows that *these principles are the most likely to enhance the growth of your wealth and minimize your risk.*

Additionally, you should be able to ask your financial advisor, "How much money did I make this past quarter, or year?" Don't be shy about asking your advisor how much he or she took in fees and commissions. In other words, get your financial advisor to simplify everything for you using a short-and-sweet bottom line.

There are plenty of other ways to ensure that your advisor is one of the good ones. It's actually not as complicated as you might think. If you have an advisor right now and want to take a step back and determine his or her value, here's what you need to evaluate:

**1. Are there any conflicts of interest between how your financial advisor is compensated and the investment strategy that is in your best interest?** In other words, does your advisor make commissions from the sale of mutual funds? And is your advisor incentivized to sell specific funds from the financial institution that employs him or her over other funds that might be better investment options, like index funds from another firm?

It would be unfair to say that all advisors who make their money from commissions on the sale of financial products and services are going to put their own financial livelihood before your best interest. It's usually not that black-and-white. But the reality is that incentives often influence people, if only at a subconscious level. When you live in a world focused primarily on high-fee investment options, you are more likely to come to believe that those options are also best for your clients. Please see "How I Cost My Clients Millions of Dollars Without Even Realizing It: Confessions of a Retired Financial Planner" in chapter 3 for more information on this phenomenon.

If your advisor's livelihood is commission-based, then be sure to take *extra* care that your fund fees are reasonable and that he or she is sticking to the investment strategy you discussed. You should not be getting regular calls asking for authorization to buy or sell investments—this is a red flag.

**2. Does your advisor take your *full* financial picture into account?** While advisors focus on your accounts outside of your employee benefits, your real estate, and your debt and really can't be expected to spend time with you on how to best manage these areas of your finances, a good advisor should be aware of your overall financial picture. There's no reason to share the details of all your credit card charges for the month, but your advisor should have a general idea of your net worth (including the amount of your debt as well as your home equity and other major assets), how you are investing in your company's retirement plan, and the value of any key employee benefits you have, like stock options, traditional pension plans, and balances in your HSA. Any advisor who *does not* ask you questions about your overall financial situation is probably costing you money.

Advisors cannot create a tax-efficient portfolio without knowing your overall financial picture, nor can they ensure that they are effectively managing your risk by compensating for areas where you may be heavily invested in specific assets. In addition, they are unlikely to truly understand you, your goals, and your needs—which makes them basically financial service salespeople, not legitimate financial planners who work with you to build your wealth.

**3. Are your financial advisor's recommendations always consistent with the investment strategy that you both agreed to based on your situation and goals?** If it's clear that you are a conservative investor, your advisor should not be recommending technology-related mutual funds or even small company (small-cap) growth funds; at most, such a recommendation should be offered for only a very small part of your portfolio and for a very strategic reason.

Consider your investment strategy your personal financial "constitution"—all of your advisor's recommendations and actions on your behalf must be "constitutional," or fully in line with your investment strategy. If they're not, it's probably time to say good-bye even if the advisor has gotten you great returns. Advisors who stray from the overall investment strategy you have established are ticking time bombs. All it takes is one market correction to find yourself in serious trouble.

**4. Does your advisor talk openly about what you can do to minimize taxes?** Financial advisors are typically not accountants, and that's okay. But there are significant tax implications for each type of account they recommend setting up, for when they buy and sell investments, for the types of investments they recommend, and for how they manage your portfolio to help you offset high taxes from selling other investments (like real estate), exercising stock options, or selling your own business. In other words, if you don't hear the word "taxes" come out of your advisor's mouth regularly, something's probably amiss. And if your advisor isn't putting you in tax-favorable accounts whenever possible, like an IRA, a 529 plan, or a Coverdell education savings account, then you most likely have the wrong financial advisor.

**5. Does your advisor bring you back to your investment strategy (or financial "constitution") when you have impulsive ideas about buying or selling investments based on how well they have performed for your friends or coworkers, or when you watch the market plummet and promptly call with instructions to "sell everything"?** If you work with an advisor long enough, conflicts should happen in the course of your discussions about your money. And that's a good thing. You do not want a yes-man or yes-woman. Otherwise, you could save the fees and do it yourself.

I wish I could tell you what the market is going to do, or which mutual funds to invest in. I'd sell far more copies of this book and be much wealthier myself if I had some sort of secret no one else has when it comes to choosing the right investments. However, if I did, I'd be lying. And to be honest, I'd deserve to be imprisoned for fraud. Sure, some people get lucky—and most of them brag profusely about their luck. But getting lucky in the market is not the norm, despite what you may hear from your know-it-all coworker or wealthy neighbor who "made a killing" in penny stocks.

The good news is that you *can* become wealthy faster than you expected by following proven principles that work—such as those outlined in this chapter—and by working with an excellent financial advisor if you are in a position to benefit from one. A 3 percent return advantage can amount to hundreds of thousands of dollars—even a million dollars—over time, putting you well ahead of the vast majority of investors. Your investment strategy may not make for an exciting cocktail party story, but it will buy you a fulfilling financial life.

Just don't make the mistake almost all of us do at some point in our lives and forget about taxes. Advisors often forget to discuss tax implications with their clients, and that can cost you dearly. In the next chapter, find out how you can avoid overpaying the IRS in taxes and why tax planning, not investing, is actually the most important thing an advisor can do for you. Tax planning is what separates a great advisor from one who can actually end up costing you money.

# 5

## Taxes: Why Your Investment Statement Is Not Entirely Accurate

**Every year millions** of investment statements go out to investors, and sadly, the majority of them overstate the amount of money investors actually have. You'd think this would be grounds for a lawsuit, but it's actually one of the more minor offenses committed by financial advisors because it's almost always completely unintentional.

Let me be clear: When I say the statements are not entirely accurate, *I don't mean they are fraudulent.* While fraud can wipe you out financially and is important enough for us to dedicate a chapter in the book to identifying bogus advisors, fraud, thankfully, is quite rare. By contrast, the overstated investment statements I'm referring to are *totally legal.*

The problem is that the returns and profits you see are *before* tax. Some statements, like those for your retirement plan, where investments grow tax-deferred, are accurate, but only until you are ready to withdraw your assets. When you do, you will have to pay taxes on whatever you withdraw. Statements are not accurate, however, for any taxable account: when you simply set up an account at a brokerage firm without putting your assets into an IRA or other tax-advantaged plan like a 529 plan, all your profits are indeed taxable. Depending on your tax bracket and how long you have held on to your investments, and provided you have made money on the investments in the previous year, the

value of your account cited on your investment statement is quite simply either a little or a lot overstated.

What does this mean? *You may not be as wealthy as you think you are.*
That's because when it comes time to pay your taxes, some portion of
the money you earned on your investments will have to go to Uncle Sam
and possibly also to your state treasurer.

Your advisor probably won't tell you this for several reasons: First,
most advisors are not accountants and do not have all the details needed
to estimate how much you will owe in taxes. Second, because everyone
has a different tax bracket and situation, there is no way any financial
institution could issue perfectly accurate after-tax statements. And
third, many advisors assume you already know about the tax implications of profits on investments, so they don't even think about mentioning it.

And indeed, you may actually know something about these implications—somewhere in the back of your mind. The problem is that far too
many people simply look at their statements to track their wealth and
forget to keep track of the tax implications . . . until it's too late.

This is a notorious problem for lottery winners. If you win a lump
sum of $1 million, you may discover it's worth about half that when taxes
are considered—by which time you may have already spent more than
you now need to pay in taxes. In any "sudden money" situation—whether
you're a professional athlete signing a multimillion-dollar contract, a per-
former earning a huge amount of money over the course of a year, someone who inherited a large sum, or even a retiree withdrawing all of your
retirement assets—you run the risk of owing a lot more in taxes than you
ever imagined and not having the cash on hand to pay the tax bill.

## THE MOST EXPENSIVE MISTAKE PEOPLE MAKE
## WHEN IT COMES TO TAXES

The tax problems that crop up in "sudden money" situations are symp-
tomatic of a much bigger problem that many people face. It's called "tax

denial," and it's a mass epidemic among the employees we work with at Financial Finesse.

By tax denial I don't mean that you're not filing a tax return. What I mean is that you are putting taxes in the back of your mind until right before they are due. You can both incur taxes and save on taxes every single day of the year, but people in tax denial (which included me through most of my twenties) don't think about taxes until they have to, and then they try to complete their tax forms as quickly as possible. Typically, they scramble to complete their taxes on April 14 or 15, rush to submit electronically, and then move on to more pleasant tasks.

Here's what happens to people in tax denial: *they make mistakes rushing to complete their tax returns at the last minute and end up missing out on important deductions.* If you don't take a tax deduction when you have earned one, the IRS is not going to call you and alert you to that fact. Basically, if you don't report it, it doesn't exist and you miss out on the full amount of the deduction.

It's very hard to estimate what the average American is overpaying in taxes by not taking key deductions and credits. Most commonly, when we work with employees who are doing their taxes at the last minute, with no help, we're able to help them find between $1,000 and $5,000 extra in tax savings. Unfortunately, these "do-it-yourselfers" are calling us as a last resort — usually to inquire about filing for an extension!

For every person who calls us, I imagine there are thousands more who don't have access to financial education through their employer and aren't using tax preparation software or services. Collectively, this lack of knowledge and guidance adds up to a large amount of money. Looking at what would happen over a lifetime if these people *invested* the money they overpaid in taxes, the annual cost of that $1,000 to $5,000 they missed out on in tax savings would grow to over $500,000 over 30 years (based on an 8 percent annual rate of return). They could have purchased a car or a home or accrued some serious Freedom Money for what they gave up by *not* taking the time to make sure they took advantage of key tax deductions and credits.

But wait, it gets worse . . .

It's obviously very important to identify all the deductions and credits for which you are eligible, but the reality is that you have the opportunity to save taxes *all year long* by taking steps to reduce your taxable income. Those in tax denial don't factor this into their financial plan . . . or their advisor doesn't. As a result, they miss out on some of the best opportunities to reduce their taxes and end up with a lot more money in their pocket:

- They don't keep receipts so that they can track business expenses that their employer doesn't reimburse.
- They open up a taxable account when they could just as easily set up an account to be tax-free.
- They invest without regard to taxes, which on average leads to paying at least twice as much in taxes on investment income than would otherwise be the case.

When you look at what good tax planning can do to keep more money in your pocket, the numbers get considerably higher than what you can save simply through careful tax preparation when it's time to file your taxes on April 15. Over the course of a lifetime, the difference between good and poor tax planning can amount to over $1 million! It's crazy to think about how some relatively simple steps to reduce your taxable income can matter that much, but they do.

## HOW TO KEEP MORE MONEY IN YOUR POCKET AND PAY LESS TO THE IRS

Let's face it. For most people, there are few things more boring than the nuances of tax law. Even worse, don't count on your financial advisor to give you some alerts on this. Yes, many will, but a lot of them will not.

With that in mind, this chapter focuses on *how you can work the tax system to your advantage*. The best thing about tax planning is that it's one of the few ways you can end up with more money without having to either make financial sacrifices or take on extra risk (provided, of course, you aren't getting too "creative" with how you interpret tax law). All you need to do is follow a few steps that you would otherwise overlook—steps that typically take relatively little time and effort but make a big difference to your financial security over time.

## Step 1: Find the right help.

The first step in saving money on taxes is probably the most important. The reality is that tax law is incredibly complicated, and to understand it the way a professional does, you'd literally have to become a professional yourself. You should know the basics about saving taxes, so you can make sure your financial advisor or tax professional is looking out for you, and you need to plan ahead if you don't have a financial advisor. Beyond that, however, it's not realistic to think you can become an expert. And it probably wouldn't be the best use of your time and talents anyway. That's why finding the right help is so important.

When you break it down, everyone has two distinct needs when it comes to taxes:

**1.** Tax planning throughout the year so that you lower your taxable income and reduce what you have to pay in taxes

**2.** Tax preparation so that you correctly file your taxes and take advantage of all the deductions and credits you are due

Tax planning and tax preparation typically require different skill sets. What follows are some guidelines on how to find the best help in each area.

*Tax Planning*

When most people think of "tax planning," they confuse it with tax preparation and think they need to hire a CPA. In reality, your financial advisor is the one who can help you most in this area. In fact, one of the hallmarks of a great financial advisor—and possibly that person's greatest value—is helping you create a very tax-efficient investment strategy. You'll discover in later chapters that one advisor cannot predict what the market will do any better than another, but the difference between what a great advisor can save you in taxes and what an "average" advisor is able to save you can be significant.

In fact, tax planning may be the primary reason for hiring an advisor, because there are so many complexities to consider if you have significant taxable income that you want to shield from taxes. You should make tax planning a key part of your selection process when you interview potential advisors. Ask them to explain exactly how they create a tax-efficient investment strategy for their clients and make sure they cover each of the following items:

**1. They establish tax-favorable accounts and trusts for their clients, with a focus on those that are totally tax-free.** That means you pay no taxes on what you contribute or on any of the earnings even when you withdraw money from the account. This is a minimum requirement. Any advisor who is not doing this for you is really a broker, whose focus is simply selling you investments, as opposed to a true financial planner.

**2. They practice tax loss harvesting.** This is another basic strategy that any good advisor uses when it makes sense. With tax loss harvesting, advisors minimize your taxable investment income by selling investments that are losing money to bring down your net profit. This is a very good strategy if you are having significant investment income and have no compelling reason to hold your losing investments.

**3. They follow a low-turnover strategy.** Your investment gains may be taxed at your ordinary income rate if you sell your investments within a year. But any investments you hold for longer than one year may get favorable tax treatment when you sell them. If they are capital assets like stocks, they are taxed at a capital gains rate, which is typically less than your ordinary income tax rate.

**4. They use accounts strategically.** Your more aggressive investments should go into your tax-free accounts because these investments are expected to grow the most over time and so should be shielded the most from taxes. By contrast, your least aggressive investments should go in taxable accounts (once you've maxed out your tax-advantaged options) because they are expected to grow less over time and will generate less taxable income as a result. In short: if it produces a lot of taxable income, hold it in a tax-advantaged account, and if it's supposed to make a lot of gains, hold it in a tax-free account first and a regular brokerage account second.

**5. They will work with your tax preparer to make sure you are fully maximizing all your tax savings when you file your taxes.** Otherwise, all the tax planning in the world won't make a great difference. Very few financial advisors also offer tax preparation services. This could be a good option for you, for both cost and simplicity, but make sure you evaluate the advisor's tax preparation skills separately based on the guidelines I provide in this section. Excellent tax planning skills don't necessarily translate into excellent tax preparation skills.

*Tax Preparation*

If you have a relatively simple tax situation (no rental properties, no businesses, no interstate or international tax issues), or if you just prefer doing it on your own, tax software is probably your best bet. If your income is below $60,000, you can qualify for the IRS's Free File Program, which lets you use leading software tax preparation programs for free. Otherwise, tax software is readily available for around $40 to $60. However, this software is likely to help you uncover deductions and credits you weren't aware of that will nicely save you enough money to cover the cost. The most popular programs are TurboTax, H&R Block, and TaxACT. There are no substantive differences between them, and choosing one is mainly about personal preference. Give them a try (you generally don't pay until you file) and see which one you like best.

*Choosing a Tax Professional*

If you're worried about making a mistake or just don't have the time or the patience to do it yourself, it's time to hire a professional tax preparer.

It's particularly important to hire someone to help you if you have a more complex tax situation, like rental properties or a business, or if you potentially owe taxes in multiple states or countries. In more complex situations, it's easy to miss valuable deductions or to get hit with interest and penalties for underpaying.

If you have one of these more complicated situations, you will probably be better off with an Enrolled Agent (EA). EAs are licensed by the IRS by either passing a comprehensive three-part IRS exam or gaining sufficient experience as a former IRS employee; all EAs have to meet continuing education and ethical standards. It's the highest credential awarded by the IRS, and an EA can represent you in an audit. You can search for a local EA through the National Association of Enrolled Agents (naea.org). Be sure to check an EA's disciplinary history with the IRS Office of Enrollment.

If you own a business, you might want to hire a CPA who specializes in tax preparation since that person is also trained in business accounting. Some CPAs have a Personal Financial Specialist (PFS) designation, indicating that they have more comprehensive financial planning expertise as well. You can search for a CPA/PFS at findacpapfs.org, and as with an EA, check the disciplinary history of anyone you're considering at your state's board of accountancy. If you're watching your costs, a CPA might be best suited to handle your business and more complicated personal tax planning and returns.

Some financial advisors also do tax preparation, and if your advisor is one of them, you can simplify your finances by having that person handle both your investments and your taxes. Bear in mind, however, that someone who is a good advisor isn't necessarily also a good tax preparer—or a good fit for your particular tax needs—so be sure to apply the same scrutiny as you would to other tax preparers.

*Working with a Tax Professional*
Regardless of which type you choose, the IRS has provided some good guidelines for working with a professional tax preparer:

- **Ask if your preparer has a Preparer Tax Identification Number (PTIN).** Any preparer who is paid for preparing and representing your tax return needs to have a PTIN; otherwise, that person is subject to penalties and disciplinary action by the IRS.
- **Make sure you understand how and what your preparer charges.** Avoid preparers who charge a percentage of the refund they can get you or who claim to get bigger refunds than others. Many of these tax preparation services are fraudulent and claim deductions or credits for which you're not eligible in order to boost their bottom line. This can get you in a lot of trouble if—or should I say when—you are audited.
- **Make sure your preparer is accessible and responsive both during and after tax season in case you have questions.**
- **Never sign a blank return or sign your return without reviewing it.** When you sign your tax return, you are attesting to its accuracy. If the numbers don't look right, they probably aren't.
- **Make sure your tax preparer signs your return too.** Ultimately you are responsible for what's on your return, but you can at least seek some money back from your preparer's bond and errors and omissions insurance if the mistake is your preparer's. Be sure to ask about this protection!
- **Make sure refunds are sent to you or your bank account, not to your preparer or anywhere else.** This is where a lot of preparer fraud starts.

### Step 2: Save all your receipts for anything that could be tax-deductible and scan them periodically so that you have an electronic copy.

One of my most vivid memories is tax-related (sad, I know). It is now over 20 years ago, but still feels like yesterday. Picture this: It was April 14 (the day before taxes were due) around 10:00 P.M., and my roommate Karen (not her real name) was starting to panic. She was finishing up her taxes, only to discover that . . . *she had lost all her receipts!* Karen's accountant had told her—and rightly so—that he wouldn't sign off on her tax return until she produced her receipts to prove that the tax-deductible business expenses she was claiming were all accounted for in the event of an audit.

So all year long she had saved every receipt for any expense that could be tax-deductible in a plastic bag. But when she went to the drawer where she kept her bag filled with receipts, it was empty! We had just hired a maid (because I was so messy), and apparently the maid had a pretty liberal definition of what she considered "trash."

You probably know where this story is going. We lived in one of those high-rise apartment buildings where you put your trash in a bag that ends up in the basement for pickup the next morning.

Karen and I sorted through virtually *every single* bag of trash from the more than 300 residents of the apartment complex (which, unfortunately, provided the "vivid" part of this most vivid memory) until we finally found the trash bag that held her plastic bag of receipts. It was dripping in soy sauce, but fortunately it was intact—holding all the receipts for over $11,000 in tax-deductible expenses, which translated into an extra $3,500 in her tax refund check.

Like so many of us do, Karen used the refund for a nice vacation rather than investing it in her future, where it could have grown to a large sum of money over time . . . but it was still a big deal to her, and understandably so. That bag of receipts was worth a week's vacation in Palm Beach.

There are two morals to this story, which I tell everyone who asks me about how to reduce their taxes: (1) save receipts for any expenses you think might be tax-deductible, because even small expenses add up over the course of a year; and (2) buy a scanner and use it regularly.

Keep receipts for all of the following expenses so that you can deduct them when you file your taxes:

- Charitable donations (including noncash donations)
- Unreimbursed business expenses (including rental property)

- Expenses for job hunting and moving for a new job (if 50 or more miles away)
- Day care expenses for family members who are under 13 or incapacitated
- Investment, legal, and tax preparation fees
- Losses from theft or casualty
- Unreimbursed medical expenses
- Overnight trips for military reservists (if more than 100 miles from home)

For more information on expenses that are tax-deductible, please go to financialfinesse.com/financialindependenceday.

## Step 3: Maximize tax-advantaged accounts.

When it comes to saving taxes, there is a general hierarchy of accounts:

**1.** Accounts that are totally tax-free

**2.** Accounts that let you withdraw all your earnings without paying taxes but do not let you claim a tax deduction on contributions

**3.** Accounts that are tax-deferred (you pay no taxes on what you earn until you begin to make withdrawals)

All three types provide you with some degree of tax savings, with the totally tax-free accounts providing the greatest savings and tax-deferred accounts providing the smallest—provided you are like the majority of people who would spend the tax deduction rather than save or invest it.

Keep in mind that what I shared in the first chapter about prioritizing your employee benefits above outside accounts applies here too, because your employer often contributes to those benefits and typically gets favorable fees. Plus, your employee benefits cover your most pressing needs—like health care and retirement. Outside accounts, even those that are totally tax-free, tend to be supplemental and focused on goals like funding college or extending your retirement savings beyond what you are already investing in your employer's retirement benefits.

*Accounts on Which You Never Pay Taxes*
The gold standard in tax savings is the totally tax-free investment account. You get a tax deduction for the money you invest, that money grows with no taxes on it while it is in the account, *and* you owe no taxes on it when you withdraw the money! Most of these accounts may be available through your employer, while some can be set up on your own. The following chart provides a summary of the accounts that require no payment of taxes on either contributions or withdrawals:

| Account | Purpose | Drawbacks | Annual Contribution Limit | Annual Tax Savings at a 25 Percent Marginal Rate | Earnings on Tax Savings Invested at 8 Percent Over 30 Years |
|---------|---------|-----------|--------------------------|-------------------------------------------------|-------------------------------------------------------------|
| Health care flexible spending account (FSA) | To cover health care expenses (limited to vision and dental if you also have an HSA) | You must use it by the end of the year or lose it. (Some plans allow you to carry over $500.) | $2,550 | $637.50 | $72,218 |
| Dependent care FSA | To cover day care, preschool, and after-school expenses | Use it by the end of the year or lose it. | $5,000 per family | $1,250 | $141,604 |

| Account | Purpose | Drawbacks | Annual Contribution Limit | Annual Tax Savings at a 25 Percent Marginal Rate | Earnings on Tax Savings Invested at 8 Percent Over 30 Years |
|---|---|---|---|---|---|
| Health savings account (HSA) | To cover health care expenses | You must pay taxes plus a 20 percent penalty if you use this account for nonqualified expenses before age 65. | Must be enrolled in an HSA-eligible high-deductible health plan: $3,350 for an individual; $6,750 for a family; plus additional $1,000 if age 55 or older (for 2016) | $837.50 or $1,087.50 if age 55 or older | $94,875 |
| Commuter benefits | To pay for transit passes, van-pool fares, and parking | | $380 per month | $1,140 | $129,143 |

Note: Limits are for 2015 unless otherwise indicated.

*Accounts That Let You Withdraw Earnings Without Paying Taxes*
Other types of tax-sheltered accounts and investments don't reduce your federal taxes when you put the money in, but the money can then grow tax-free. Although these accounts won't save you as much in taxes in the short term, you can end up with more savings in the long run, since you can generally contribute more money and leave it to grow for a longer period of time.

*Accounts That Defer Taxes*
Lastly, there are accounts that are tax-deferred, like traditional IRAs and pretax employer-sponsored retirement plans. You don't pay taxes when

you put the money in, but you do pay taxes when you take it out. So how is that a benefit if you still have to pay taxes on it?

For starters, you might be in a lower tax bracket when you retire. For example, a single person earning $50,000 of income in 2015 would be in the 25 percent marginal tax bracket. Assuming that person only needs 80 percent of their income in retirement, their $40,000 income would drop them into the 15 percent marginal tax bracket.

But what if you retire in the same tax bracket? There's still the advantage of tax-deferred growth. Consider the following two investors:

Jacob invests $10,000 in a taxable account earning 5 percent interest. At the end of the first year, he would have $10,375. That's because he would owe $125 in tax on the $500 of interest earned (assuming a 25 percent tax rate). At the end of 30 years, Jacob's $10,000 investment would be worth $30,175.

Carrie invests $10,000 in a tax-deferred account also earning 5 percent interest. At the end of the first year, she would have $10,500, since taxes are deferred. At the end of 30 years, Carrie would have $43,220, of

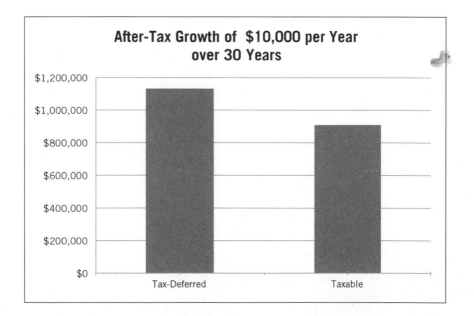

which $33,220 is interest that has not been taxed yet. If she is also in the 25 percent tax bracket, the after-tax value of Carrie's $10,000 investment would be $34,915. That's $4,740 more than Jacob's!

## Step 4: Manage your tax preparer or financial advisor.

Tax help can be a lifesaver, but if you don't manage your professionals properly, you automatically limit their effectiveness. Here are some guidelines you can follow to get the best out of your tax preparation service as well as your financial advisor.

*Managing Your Tax Preparer*

For whatever reason, people tend to think their tax preparer is psychic — that somehow their preparer simply knows the ins and outs of their financial lives. Obviously, a good tax preparer will ask as many questions as possible, but he or she can't help you if you don't have the answers. Also, it is your job to bring up anything you have done over the year to minimize your taxes so that your preparer can take that into account when filing your taxes. And perhaps most importantly, as noted at the beginning of the chapter, your advisor must be part of the tax preparation process, since he or she has a full record of all your investments and what specifically was done to shield them from taxes. You don't want your tax preparer to miss anything that could save you money on taxes, so it's critical to make sure he or she has all the necessary information.

*Managing Your Financial Advisor*

**1. When you hire a financial advisor, tell that person that tax-efficient investing is important to you and ask him or her to prioritize maximizing your after-tax profits (or returns).** Most people think that their advisor knows this already, but when you stress it, you send an important signal. You are letting your advisor know that (1) you understand the importance of tax planning, and (2) you will be holding him or her accountable not just for what you see on your statement but for the net returns.

Think of hiring an advisor as something like getting a haircut or being fitted for a new suit. If the hairdresser and tailor you are working with know that you are turning to them because it's your wedding day and everything must be perfect, they will use more diligence than if you simply waltz in like it's a regular day in your life. They would never try to give you a bad haircut or a badly tailored suit, but their level of focus will be higher if they know how important what they are doing is to you — and they are likely to expend extra time and effort on getting it "just right." Same thing with financial advisors.

**2. Follow up by sharing your last year's tax return with your advisor and note any changes in income, so that he or she understands your tax bracket.** This way, your advisor can calculate the after-tax return on your investments and show you, in real numbers, how much you are saving as a result of working together on tax planning.

**3. Keep your advisor abreast of any changes to your situation.** Your advisor needs to know if you get a raise that might affect your tax bracket, if you have a child, or if you get married or divorced (or are even just considering it). In fact, you should tell your advisor about any major life change you are either considering or in the midst of navigating.

Almost every life change has some sort of tax implications and could be a trigger for your advisor to revisit your tax planning strategy. If you've gotten married or had a child, perhaps you need more life insurance — and you want a permanent policy that is tax-free. Permanent or whole life policies are expensive but worth it in the right situation. If you've received a significant raise, it may be time for your advisor to put you in tax-free municipal bonds, which typically give high-net-worth investors an edge when it comes to their net returns.

• • •

Taxes are not fun—not even for me, and I was in the math club in high school! But it is incredible how much money you can save by taking the right steps both to plan and to prepare your taxes, and how much that savings can affect your financial security over time. Far too many people are leaving money on the table when it comes to their taxes. Don't be one of them. Life is too short to be spending it in tax denial.

# 6

---

## Your Life Partner May Be Your
## Worst Financial Enemy

**The person you** spend your life with will matter much more to your financial security, and ultimately to how wealthy you become, than anything any financial advisor can do for you. And I'm not just warning you about "gold diggers."

The person you marry or spend your life with can be your best financial friend . . . or your worst financial enemy. You can have a partner who has a boatload of money and can buy you financial security, but is not your best financial friend. And you can have a partner who makes a minimum-wage salary and has poor prospects for advancement, but is not your financial enemy. More importantly, the person you spend your life with will influence you every day in how you save, spend, invest, and protect your money. And over time the difference between managing your money exceptionally well as a couple—or even doing just average—and not managing it well can be worth millions.

And this doesn't even include those who choose a partner who has destructive financial habits. This is a disaster waiting to happen. Yes, you can recover from investment losses, or even job losses, but a partner who ruins your credit, raids your accounts, or leaves you with a mountain of debts when he or she dies is much more devastating—and it can take much longer to recover both emotionally and financially.

## WHY YOUR FINANCIAL ADVISOR NEVER
## TALKS ABOUT RELATIONSHIPS AND FINANCES

So if who you choose to spend your life with is so important to your financial security, then why don't advisors stress this more? Why do many advisors actually avoid working with couples, preferring instead to work with just one partner in a couple and treating that person as the "representative" of the couple's wishes?

There are several reasons financial advisors ignore the impact of relationships on finances:

**1. Financial advisors are not marriage counselors.** They don't have the skills, training, or patience to facilitate productive discussions with a couple about their money. They are there to invest your assets, and it's easiest for them when they can work with one person rather than two, who might often disagree as to the right course of action.

**2. They don't look at your finances holistically.** Financial advisors aren't compensated to help you with the issues that couples struggle with the most: the financial and emotional trade-offs associated with balancing work and home; what to spend money on and what to forgo or delay; how much debt to take on, from what sources, and how quickly to pay it off; when to buy a car or a home; when to have a child; . . . The list goes on. Every day you and your spouse, either jointly or separately, make decisions about money. A financial advisor isn't going to pop up in your living room or accompany you to the store when you have to make decisions both small and large about how to spend your money.

**3. They don't want to get involved in your relationship.** Financial advisors don't want to know the details of how you make financial decisions as a couple, and they certainly don't want to play referee or, worse, discuss with either of you how expensive your partnership actually is. That would be a very quick way to get fired.

Every partnership has either a net financial cost or a net financial profit. Sometimes these costs or profits are large enough to be glaringly obvious; other times they're more subtle. Because advisors don't want to get involved, these net costs and profits are never calculated, and couples go on with their lives, either building financial security or losing it, based on the dynamics of their relationship. Thus, one of the most important aspects of financial planning is ignored, and unfortunately, most partnerships never realize their full financial potential.

If you are in a relationship, consider this chapter a step-by-step guide to help you make the best possible financial decisions together, so that you can harness your respective strengths and build wealth much faster as a team than you could individually.

## Step 1: Determine how your relationship is affecting your finances.

Obviously, if you are in a relationship and you and your partner combine finances, your partner's actions will have more impact on your financial security than if you keep separate accounts. Similarly, if you and your partner have taken the step of entering into a marriage or domestic partnership, there's more connection between your spouse's finances and your own than there was before you did so. All that said, any relationship can have an impact on your finances. Whatever kind of relationship you are in (or considering), it's worth examining whether the relationship is helping you build your financial security or simply draining it.

There are a lot of ways to examine this question, but it comes down to one basic calculation: are you better off financially because you are in this relationship than you would be on your own?

This calculation is not nearly as simple as you may think. You have to really take a step back and look past the value of the "gifts" you give each other or the money you each contribute to your joint account. In almost every relationship, there's one partner who earns more, but that isn't what you should be focused on. What matters is your partner's long-term financial impact on your relationship. If your partner is the main breadwinner, does he or she work with you to ensure that you are growing your combined wealth over time and achieving key financial goals in the process? Or does your partner take the breadwinner role as a license to reward himself or herself?

If you earn the same amount, are you supporting each other to achieve key career goals? Or are you competing with each other and ending up in a dangerous game of one-upmanship, focusing more on out-earning (and potentially outspending) each other? Does your partner inspire you to make good career and financial decisions, or does he or she influence you to make impulsive purchases and investments that you later regret? Are you more or less financially responsible because of your partner? Or are you more or less financially stressed?

If, as in my case, your spouse is not the main breadwinner but takes primary responsibility for caring for your children, your home, and ultimately your personal life outside of work, then you know how absolutely invaluable that role can be. I am a much better CEO because my husband is in my life. In fact, my business has grown 10-fold since I married him in 2005. He brings me perspective that I wouldn't otherwise have and provides a sanctuary when work is draining and I'm flirting with burnout. Most importantly, he takes care of things at home so I can be present and focused at work, knowing that our son, our dogs, and our overall life are in great hands. We have reached every single turning point in our business owing, either directly or indirectly, to his unflagging support.

Conversely, because I am able to provide for us and have a thriving business, he is financially better off than he would be going it alone and resuming his career in financial services as a single person. Both of us are better off because of our respective contributions to the relationship.

On the flip side, the story would have been far different if I had married a previous boyfriend who always wanted to control the finances. The more I complained about the situation, the more he'd spend out of a sense of righteousness. (Initially I'd been drawn to his independent, rebellious streak.) I felt like I had to limit myself and not surpass him career-wise, and if I'd stayed with him, I probably would never have even started my own business. Now that business is the biggest source of my family's wealth. Both of us would have been worse off—especially when you factor in the cost of therapy and divorce!

The point is, every couple usually develops a pattern early on as to how they are going to handle money—who's going to pay the monthly bills, who's going to watch over investments, etc. It's certainly fine if one of the partners steps up and handles all that, but it's also essential that both individuals are up to speed on their joint money and investments. This is a team effort, and it's important that both of you know what's going on with your money.

### Step 2: If there's a problem, determine whether it lies with your partner or with the way you are managing your money together.

Even in the healthiest relationships, couples will sometimes disagree over how to spend, save, invest, or protect their money. In that moment, you'll feel like your partner is the problem. If he or she could just *understand* the right way to handle this situation, you think, you'd both be much better off! It's totally natural to go through this when you disagree about a financial decision. Disagreeing now and then, however, doesn't mean that your partner is financially irresponsible. It simply means that you disagree and need to work through the issue together. If you have shared goals and priorities, you're likely to arrive at a solution that you can both get behind and then move on.

When I ask if the problem is your partner or your partnership, I'm really asking if your partner is financially irresponsible on an ongoing basis. Does your partner have a compulsive spending or gambling problem? Is your partner unable to face the problem and get the help he or she needs?

Ideally, you need to make sure that your partner is financially responsible before you get married—and certainly before you combine finances. Most people think they can make this assessment simply by observing how their partner spends his or her money, but this often leads to the mistake of thinking that your significant other is financially secure because he or she has the material trappings of success. In fact, "living the high life" is often a red flag. What you may not realize is that your partner is significantly overextended and financing a life that he or she can't afford. If this is the case, you will have to contend with high levels of debt if you marry this person or if you combine your finances, and that can be a weighty drain on your ability to grow your wealth.

Even for couples who have been together for a while, the *only* way to know for sure that the love of your life is financially responsible is to have the "money talk." This is when both partners openly share all aspects of their financial lives, right down to the nitty-gritty of how much debt each partner has, both partners' credit scores and any issues with credit, how much each partner has saved for emergencies, how each has invested money for long-term goals, and both partners' current monthly income and expenses.

Yes, this is an extremely difficult conversation to have. But it's a very important one. In truth, the vast majority of couples skirt this conversation or gloss over it with mutual assurances that they have their finances under control. In doing so, they put themselves, their relationship, and their finances in a precarious position. Consider Sarah's story, which is representative of stories we hear almost every day from people whose "better half" completely decimated them financially.

Sarah knew Todd had some credit card debt before they married, but she had a knack for saving and investing money and actually saw the situation as an opportunity to help him—and also, ironically, as a sign that they were good together.

What Sarah didn't know until after they were married and had twin sons was that Todd had much more credit card debt than she ever imagined. He was maxed out on seven credit cards and falling further behind on his monthly payments. When he stopped being able to get credit, he used their joint account to keep funding the lifestyle he'd grown accustomed to. In a single month, he blew through most of their savings, hiding purchases by having big-ticket items delivered to his friend's house. Sarah found out only when her mortgage check bounced—at which point the couple was in dire straits financially.

Eventually Sarah gave Todd an ultimatum: get a second job to help pay off their debts and rebuild their savings or leave. But he flat-out refused, saying that they were doing okay and would get through this down time. Stunned and distraught, Sarah filed for divorce.

In the end, Sarah was stuck with all the bills, the mortgage, and a large attorney bill. Her credit score had been trashed, and she was probably going to lose her house in foreclosure.

As it turned out, Sarah's story carries one clear and important warning: having that financial talk with your partner is absolutely essential.

What other lessons can you take from Sarah's story?

**1. Marrying or combining finances with someone who is financially irresponsible can devastate your own finances.** Before you take either of these steps, you need to know the person's financial situation down to the penny.

**2. Don't just take your partner's word for it.** Set the example by taking the time to share your finances in detail—the good, the bad, and the ugly—and ask your partner to do the same. Show each other your credit reports, bank and investment statements, every single credit card statement, and exactly how you are spending your money.

**3. Do not end this conversation until you have a clear understanding of your partner's net worth (what is owned minus what is owed), your partner's credit score, and your partner's monthly income and expenses.** If your partner does not have a positive net worth, a strong credit score, and a spending plan for living within his or her means, understand that you are putting yourself at risk and probably should delay getting married or combining finances until your partner resolves these financial problems. Ultimately, if your partner is unable to resolve financial problems—or worse, sinks deeper into them and expects you to help him or her recover—then it's probably time to move on, unless you are truly able and willing to support your partner and can do so without jeopardizing your own financial security. Bear in mind, however, that many marriages in this country, especially younger couples in their twenties and thirties, end up falling apart because of financial woes.

One concluding note regarding Sarah: the old adage "You can't change people" very much applies here. Sarah thought she could change Todd, and that was actually a major part of what attracted her to him — the evidence of his financial irresponsibility made her feel special, like she was exactly what he needed in his life. The problem is that people change only when they are ready to change. You can't expect that the problems that exist before you combine finances are going to disappear once you do. In reality, those problems will probably get worse. In addition, the stress of a new marriage can trigger a compulsive spender to spend even more, especially when that person gets access through a joint account to money he or she didn't have before.

*Easy to Say, Hard to Do*
As I write this, I can imagine how you might be feeling.

After all, who am I to suggest all these financial guidelines for you and questions about your loved one when I know nothing about you, your partner, or any of the extenuating circumstances?

And you are right. I don't know your situation, and it is easy for me to remove myself and look at things analytically because I have no emotional attachment to you or your partner.

All I can say is that deciding who you spend your life with is likely to be not only the most important decision you'll make in your life but also the most accurate predictor of your financial security. And I can give you the best advice I ever got: before you commit your life to someone, and certainly before you combine finances, you have to be certain you can take the bad with the good.

Everyone has faults, but this decision is about choosing a partner whose faults you can accept, having determined that you can handle the impact of your partner's mistakes, emotionally and financially. I'm not suggesting that you hold out for perfection, but simply that you make sure you know what you are signing up for, so to speak, and that you can live with the consequences. If the answer is not a resounding yes, my advice is to not combine finances—or to find a way to separate your accounts (at least going forward), if you haven't already taken that step.

*My Story*
I ended two serious relationships because as much as I loved each man, I could not say, with confidence, that I could accept his faults and the consequences of his behavior for my life and our future. As I mentioned earlier, the trouble in one of those relationships was directly financial in nature—it was important for him to earn more than me and to control how our money was spent. My career was going well, however, and I knew I couldn't accept a relationship in which I had to squelch my ambitions and surrender control of our finances to my partner.

The trouble in the other relationship was indirectly financial—my partner was a lost soul and didn't know what he wanted to be when he grew up. This indecision extended to money as well—he resisted planning for the longer term because he wanted just to "see how things played out." I had a plan and knew I would regret abandoning it, and I also knew that this difference between us would become a bigger problem in our relationship over time.

The third time was the charm for me, when I met the man who would become my husband. He wasn't perfect, and that included disagreeing with me sometimes about how to spend money. But I felt that I could live with those differences and that we could manage them comfortably by having a joint account that paid for shared expenses and maintaining separate accounts to finance our individual priorities. I also knew I could trust him to be honest about everything financial. And yes, we had a painful, but important, money talk: he was willing to share all the details of his situation, I did the same, and we both learned where the skeletons were in our respective closets.

While that talk wasn't any fun, and we were both judgmental and defensive at times throughout the experience, we came away realizing that we were both financially responsible, and that we could accept and respect each other's differences when it came to money. In short, neither of us would be entering a marriage with the need to change the other.

## Step 3: Create a powerful financial partnership.

I'd like to address the elephant in the bedroom here. If you are reading this, there's a good chance you are already married or you and your partner are already combining all your finances. If you are like most couples, you probably didn't have the "money talk" before you took this step. We work every day with people who discovered only *after* they combined finances that their partner was not nearly as financially responsible as they thought. Others realized that they had absolutely no clue how well or poorly they were doing financially—having delegated the entire responsibility for managing the household finances and investments to their spouse.

If this is your situation, all is not lost. It's not too late to get on the right track financially with your partner, as long as both of you are willing to do the work. Although you cannot change another person, you can set up ways to work around your partner's weaknesses and even channel his or her strengths—so that you minimize the negative impact on your financial security and turn a financially draining partnership into a financially lucrative one. Here's what you can do, starting today:

**1. Have the money talk ASAP.** Consider taking a day off work and having someone babysit the children (if necessary) so you can totally focus on your finances without any distractions. Before you begin, set some ground rules:

> **Rule #1:** *No secrets, now or going forward.* Make a pact that you will both be totally and completely honest and open about all your

finances, both during the money talk and during the regular financial discussions you will set up after it. Let your partner know that you consider financial infidelity—such as withholding information or lying about your finances—a form of betrayal as serious as physical cheating.

**Rule #2:** *Agree to leave the past in the past and focus on the future.* You can't go back in time and undo mistakes, such as racking up a lot of debt or spending on impulsive items. But you can find the lessons in those mistakes and make sure that you operate differently going forward. As long as you are alive, you have a second chance to do things differently. Forgive yourself for what you've done wrong as well as your partner for his or her mistakes, and focus on creating a plan that will maximize your wealth from this day forward.

**Rule #3:** *Show up.* As the day of the money talk approaches, you'll find yourself thinking of all the reasons to put it on hold or to stick to safe topics. Being "financially naked" is one of the most difficult, vulnerable things you can do, especially if you aren't in great financial shape. The temptation to avoid the talk can be overwhelming. But any time you're tempted to put off the talk, think of how it would feel to be divorced because of your finances, or widowed without enough money to support yourself and your children. If you are already under financial pressure, imagine that pressure intensifying until you have to make decisions that affect your family's quality of life or, worse, your children's future. You owe it to yourself and to your family to be financially open and financially faithful. Without that, you put the people you love the most at risk.

**2. Set your financial goals and make a plan to achieve them.** There's an old saying, "If you don't know where you are going, you will never get there." Studies show that most couples do not formally set financial goals, nor do they regularly track their financial progress together. As a result, most end up scrambling to fund life's most important expenses and either come up short or take on too much debt in the process. When you have a partner for the long haul, you are on a journey together to create the life you want as a couple, and money plays a huge role in building that life.

The first step in setting goals is to discuss what you want out of life — for yourself and your children. Do you want to own a home? Or do you want to sell your current home and purchase a nicer home in a better neighborhood or school district? Is education a huge priority for you because you see it as the way to give your children the greatest opportunity to succeed in life? If so, you may want to focus on saving for private school education in addition to college. Is owning your own business a lifelong dream and one you would deeply regret giving up?

Every person and every couple has different goals. Get all yours down on paper, and then begin prioritizing them. Decide which goal is the most important, which one is second, third, and so on. Once you have your list of goals written down, set a time frame for when you want to achieve each goal and then put together a plan for *how* you are going to do it. How much are you going to need to save? How will you invest those savings? Is there a tax-free, tax-deductible, or tax-deferred account available that will enable you to grow your money faster? What expenses, if anything, do you and your spouse need to cut today?

Use the answers to questions like these to develop your plan, and then set up automatic transfers from either your paychecks or checking account to fund these goals.

Next, discuss your financial aspirations individually and as a couple. Please note that aspirations generally take a backseat to goals. Aspirations are what we really *want* to have or to do but can live without and are willing to sacrifice if needed to achieve more important financial goals. There may be times when you have only a little room to accommodate your aspirations and you'll have to get creative in finding ways to enjoy your favorite hobbies and creature comforts within a limited budget. Other times, especially if you have done a good job of saving and investing your money, you may find that you're ready to integrate your aspirations into your lifestyle. The point is to always remember—goals first, aspirations second.

Another point about aspirations is equally important—in a partnership, each of you makes a commitment to *honor* the other's aspirations whether or not you understand or agree with them.

Finally, you must carve out room in the budget to allow each of you to spend money on your aspirations. It might not be a lot if money is tight, but both you and your partner need to have "fun" money to use as you see fit. The ideal way to do this, as we'll see later, is for each of you to set up a separate account for these expenses.

### I've Been There, and It's Not Easy

Setting goals and making a plan to achieve them is not an easy process. There will probably be moments (or a series of moments) when you think your significant other is from another planet. You won't be able to get your head wrapped around the way your partner thinks or feels about certain issues, many of them being the Big Issues, and most of them having some financial element.

For Joe and me, it's always a battle of "stuff" versus "experiences." I place an unusually low value on material things, and he's the opposite. He remembers where and when he purchased everything he owns; it's as though his stuff is a part of him. Honestly, if we ever had a fire and his stuff went up in smoke, he'd be depressed for I don't know how long and probably scarred forever. I'd curse the inconvenience of having to collect the insurance, move to a new place, and furnish it, but there's nothing tangible besides family photos or other items with true sentimental value that I would mourn. I will never understand why Joe spends so much money on cars, electronics, and even video games. (Yes, we have a basement of old-school 1980s video games.) To me it's silly, and I can't help compounding in my head how much money he'd have if he'd invested it instead. But for Joe, his stuff carries great meaning.

On the other hand, I love experiences—great vacations, parties, and events that bring friends and family together and build memories that you cherish forever. To not celebrate life, to me, is to miss out on living it. And I'm okay paying a goodly amount for an important celebration. Joe, on the other hand, looks at experiences as fleeting, unlike actual possessions that you can keep forever. Even after 13 years together, he still shakes his head in disbelief when I tell him what I'm spending on an experience that, in his mind, will vanish after it happens.

All that said, despite our differences, we give each other the space to pursue our dreams, so long as those dreams don't compromise our longer-term goals. And our relationship is much better for it.

**3. Set up three bank accounts: ours, yours, and mine.** This leads to my next point: notice that when I talk about how Joe and I spend money differently, I'm talking about us as *individuals,* not as a couple. I'm astounded that Joe chooses to spend so much money on his "guy stuff," but it's *his* money from his own account. He's earned this money, and thus he gets to decide how to spend it. Same thing with the money I have in my account—this is my money to spend the way I see fit.

I recommend that, if possible, a couple should have three accounts— ours, yours, and mine. "Our" account is for joint expenses, and both people in the relationship must agree on how to spend this money. The other two accounts are individually owned, managed, and directed. It's a lot easier to tolerate someone else's spending habits when they are footing the bills for those expenses. This is understandably not always possible, especially when both incomes are needed to pay all of the bills. But a similar effect can be achieved by setting aside cash each month for each person's individual goals and aspirations.

**4. Focus on each other's strengths and set up financial roles and a system for managing your money that leverages these strengths.** Take time with your spouse to share the good, the bad, and the ugly when it comes to your financial management skills and ask him or her to do the same. Then take a step back and look at what you each can do, based on your strengths, to best support the relationship financially and compensate for the other person's weaknesses.

All of us have financial strengths and weaknesses. Those who think of themselves as "nonfinancial" types—who eschew numbers and avoid them whenever possible—may actually be great long-term planners who can visualize the life they want to build and stay motivated to work toward that goal. Those who like to take charge and are detail-oriented may relish the sense of control that comes from paying the bills at the end of the month to make sure everything is in order. Some people, like my husband, are super shoppers—excellent at finding exceptional deals and thrilled whenever they do.

And then there are the things we're not so good at. I cannot fill out a form without having a mini–panic attack. Most of the time I completely skip over key parts of the form, defeating the purpose of filling it out in the first place. My husband has a hard time planning for the long term. He knows it's important to do, but can't easily visualize what life will look like in five, 10, 20, or 30 years. I do the long-term planning and set our overall spending limits; he does the shopping, pays the bills, and fills out all the necessary forms. As a couple, we are stronger for filling these financial roles because we complement each other. I can't quantify how much better off we are financially because we play to our strengths, but I know we do significantly better than we would if we did not.

**5. Set up regular money meetings with your spouse or partner.** These meetings should happen at least once a month, more often if you are going through significant financial challenges. This typically works best if you set a regular day and time so that the meeting becomes part of your normal routine. It also helps you get into the right mind-set if you know that, say, on Sunday evenings after the kids go to bed you are going to discuss any financial issues you have or decisions you need to make. This way you can start the week or the month off having both agreed to a clear plan going forward.

### Step 4: Financially protect your relationship.

Marion and Nick had a good marriage. Nick took care of the finances, but he and Marion met regularly to discuss their financial goals and review their progress toward meeting their goals. It was a system that served them well, from buying their first home to saving for their children's college educations, to being on track for retirement. Nick had been married before, so he was very conscious of the importance of making this second marriage work, and he took extra pains to make sure he and Marion were on the same page.

Then one day, without any warning, Nick, just 50 years old, collapsed at a friend's party. He had suffered a heart attack, and within minutes he was gone. After the funeral, Marion called Nick's financial advisor and discovered that she was not the beneficiary on his Rollover IRA, which was the primary source of their savings. Ironically, his ex-wife was still listed as the beneficiary—despite the fact that they had divorced 15 years before!

Apparently Nick never even thought about this mix-up; he was so focused on accumulating wealth for himself and Marion that he didn't realize that in all those years he never changed his IRA beneficiary. Marion then called the life insurance company, only to find out that their term life insurance had expired a couple months before—something Nick was planning to rectify but never got around to. As a stay-at-home mom, she was left with their joint checking account, a small balance in a 401(k) from Nick's new job prior to his death, and the equity in their home, which wasn't much. She was forced to sell the house, move in with her elderly parents, and find a job after being out of the workforce for over 15 years.

The deep tragedy of this story is that Nick and Marion spent a lot of time and energy on their finances and did almost everything right. The mistakes they made came down to simple paperwork! Had Nick changed his beneficiary designation on his IRA at any point after he and Marion got married, she would have inherited the full balance—about $1.6 million. Had he renewed his life insurance policy or switched to permanent insurance—which would probably have been more appropriate for this situation—Marion would have had another $1 million of insurance coverage. Working with a good financial advisor, she could have set herself up to fully replace Nick's income for the rest of her life and still have a nice nest egg to rely on for unexpected expenses.

Hindsight, as they say, is 20/20, but if there is a silver lining in any of this, it's that you can learn from Marion's story. Make sure that you and your partner don't fall into the trap of forgetting to take care of what may seem like "small details" but in reality are the very things that can secure your financial future if the unthinkable were to happen.

Fortunately, protecting yourself and your partner and loved ones from financial disaster is relatively easy to do. To ensure that your finances are fully protected, you and your partner need to take the following steps:

**1. Make sure you have listed each other as the beneficiary on *all* accounts.** This includes your retirement plan at work, your life insurance, investment and savings accounts, and real estate—basically anything and everything you want to automatically pass on to your partner in the event of your death. Many people think these items need to be covered by a will, but the reality is that a simple form designating the beneficiary of your assets will do the trick. The best part is that this process avoids probate—the legal process governing the distribution of assets after a person dies, which can take six to 12 months or longer. If you designate someone as a beneficiary of one of your accounts, that person will get access to the money in that account immediately after your death. That's obviously important if your loved ones need cash to pay bills right away.

**2. Make sure you are adequately insured in all of the following areas so that unexpected accidents or events don't put you and your partner in a difficult financial situation:**

- *Long-term care insurance:* Even though an estimated 70 percent of people who reach age 65 will require some form of long-term care and the average stay in a nursing home runs about $70,000 per year, only 16 percent of people over the age of 55 report having long-term care insurance in place, according to the results of our financial wellness assessment. Get this insurance now before it becomes too expensive or you develop a medical condition that disqualifies you.

- *Health insurance:* Make sure you are appropriately covered based on your medical history as well as your family's medical history. Purchase insurance that is likely to minimize your total expenses, taking into consideration both premiums and expected out-of-pocket expenses. Calculate your worst-case scenario when deciding on an insurance policy so that you can make sure it wouldn't decimate your finances. Also, if you have a health savings account, make sure you contribute as much to it as you can—those dollars are tax-deductible, tax-deferred, and, if spent on health care, tax-free. An HSA not only helps you cover unexpected medical expenses but also can provide you with additional financial security in retirement.
- *Home and auto insurance:* In many states, it's illegal not to have home or auto insurance. Don't go cheap here, especially if you have a lot invested in your home or car.
- *Life insurance:* If your partner is the sole or primary breadwinner and you rely on that income, or vice versa, life insurance can be critically important—especially if you or your partner is limited in terms of other assets. A general rule of thumb is to purchase a policy that provides 15 times the salary of the partner who is the sole or primary breadwinner.

**3. Get a will or trust in place to ensure that your partner receives everything else you want him or her to receive if something happens to you.** If you have children, use a will or trust to assign guardianship of your children should something happen to you and your partner. Note that a trust is more appropriate if you have significant assets as a couple. A will is a better solution if your financial situation is more straightforward. To set up a will, go to nolo.com. To learn about the difference between wills and trusts, go to financialfinesse.com /financialindependenceday.

**4. Have an advance health care directive in place so that your partner isn't put in the difficult position of having to make medical decisions on your behalf if you become incapacitated.** This last step is very important, but the vast majority of people ignore it because it is so unpleasant to think about or discuss. An advance health care directive spells out your wishes regarding end-of-life care. Knowing what you want ahead of time makes decisions much easier for your loved ones. This document can also protect your nest egg if you don't want expensive end-of-life care to delay the inevitable and would rather ensure that your partner and other loved ones receive that money. To set up an advance health care directive and file it electronically, go to mydirectives.com.

### Step 5: When the time is right, work together with a good financial advisor who can help you grow your money and secure your future.

The purpose of this chapter has been to show you that an advisor cannot help you build a financially productive relationship with your partner, but he or she can help you invest your money once you've built that relationship yourself. After you have built a strong financial foundation, paid off your high-interest-rate debts, and maxed out your employee benefits, it's time to consider an advisor who can help you create and stick to a solid investment plan for the savings you've built as a couple and will continue to accumulate.

Oddly, the biggest mistake couples make is not doing this together. One person hires, manages, and actively communicates with the advisor, while the other knows very little about it, possibly nothing at all. This is arguably another kind of financial infidelity, and it's a huge problem for many couples when they divorce—often one spouse has no idea how much money they actually have! Don't let this happen to you. As part of your commitment to each other and to your relationship, make sure you select and manage your financial advisor together.

Here are four guidelines to follow when you and your partner begin working with an outside financial advisor:

**1. Select your advisor together, using the information in chapter 8 to guide you in finding a good advisor.** If you don't both give an advisor a strong thumbs-up, keep looking. The partner who feels unable to connect or communicate well with the advisor is likely to shut down, and this would become a major problem.

**2. Before you meet with your financial advisor, have all of your financial goals and associated time frames outlined.** When you have your priorities and goals already set up, your advisor can work with you and your partner on setting the appropriate investment strategies, accounts, and ongoing contributions to achieve your goals within your time frame.

**3. Both of you should attend all meetings, and both of you should receive all communications and financial statements.** Both of you need to be fully aware of what your advisor is doing and informed about its impact on your overall financial security. If anything happens to one of you or to your partnership, you'll be grateful to know what is going on with your finances and how to access your different accounts.

**4. Both you and your partner should agree to any major changes in your investment or insurance strategy.** This is part of staying informed and on top of things, but it also adds a layer of protection: two heads often think better than one, and if both of you must agree to major changes, the risk of either of you doing something impulsive and regretting it later is reduced.

Our finances are fluid, changing every day based on what we earn, spend, and save and on how our investments perform. Over the short term, luck plays a huge role, but as the days stretch into weeks and the weeks stretch into years, how you and your partner manage your money will be the number one predictor of whether your finances flourish or flounder. How you've managed your finances in the past provides lessons, but it's a waste of time and energy to linger there. What matters is what you do from this point on. We've worked with thousands of couples to transform their relationship from financially devastating to financially rewarding. In the most extreme cases, they have gone from bankruptcy to financial security by working together to start over, rebuild, and reclaim the life they always wanted.

My hope is that this chapter has given you the fundamental building blocks to create a financially healthy relationship with your partner by showing you how to get the best out of a financial advisor and how important it is that you and your partner communicate with each other on financial matters.

The good news is that after you get on the same page with your partner and establish the kind of relationship that enhances your financial security, there's a wealth-building strategy you can employ whether you choose to use a financial advisor or go it alone. It's called "automation," and it's something you may not hear financial advisors talk about very often because they worry about being replaced by services that automate the wealth-building process. The reality is that today, with or without an advisor, you can become an automatic millionaire. Read more in the next chapter to learn how.

# 7

## Become an Automatic Millionaire
## Without an Advisor's Help

**What's next is** the easy part, the part that I love. In this chapter, you'll learn how to set yourself up for success by automating a process that would otherwise require a lot of effort and sacrifice.

Can you imagine proactively saving $300 a month? For how many months do you think you would do that? Speaking for myself, any proactive savings plan would last about three months, and then I'd simply forget to set the money aside or decide I'd get to it later . . . and later would never happen. That's the reality of the lives we lead—things simply fall between the cracks. This is particularly true about things that are not easy to do, like saving money, paying off debt, or investing in your future. When money feels tight already, you can be bombarded with temptation to spend the money you meant to save or invest on things you want for yourself and your family *right now*.

Why wouldn't every financial advisor be telling clients to set up automatic payments? After all, if clients automatically invest money each month, wouldn't that be a good thing for advisors? Absolutely. And many advisors will encourage or help their clients get enrolled in an automatic investment plan. The problem is that an automatic investing process is only one piece of the pie, just as doing squats or eating breakfast every morning are only two of the activities involved in staying fit. The rest of the automation you need to put in place in your financial life either has nothing to do with advisors or could even make you question their value as you move forward.

I worked with our planners at Financial Finesse to create the following step-by-step guide you can begin using today to start technologically automating your finances. You'll learn not only what aspects of your financial life you can automate but also the impact of that one step on your wealth over time. We recommend dedicating a full day to getting all of your finances automated—maybe at your regular meeting with your significant other. Whether or not you're in a relationship, declare a Financial Independence Day and get it all done while you're motivated. Then you can move on, knowing that you've set yourself up to be an automatic millionaire.

Earlier in the book, I discussed the concept of getting to Freedom Money. Here's a detailed plan for achieving that.

## STEP-BY-STEP GUIDE TO AUTOMATICALLY INCREASING YOUR WEALTH

### Getting to Freedom Money—Level 1

Here are the steps to being able to fund several months or even years of your life so that you don't need to depend on your current paycheck.

**1. Automate the tracking of your expenses.** When you automatically track your expenses, you know exactly what you are spending and can determine what you need to cut to increase debt payments, build an emergency savings fund, and invest to become financially secure and independent. There are tons of free online tools and apps that aggregate your accounts so that you can see all of your finances in one place and get the full picture of not only how you are spending your money but how much you have in savings, investments, total debt, etc. We suggest Mint (mint.com), as it's one of the easiest to use and it's completely free, unlike others that charge a fee. Be aware that it can take one to two hours at the beginning to fully set up all your accounts, but the time is well worth it. You can also set up automatic alerts when you go over the spending limits you've set for different products and services, as well as automatic bill-pay and warnings if you get low on savings.

**2. Do the paperwork necessary to fully fund your emergency fund.** If you do not have a fully funded emergency fund (ideally, three to six months' worth of basic expenses in a bank account), get the necessary forms from your payroll department at work to set up a special transfer of a portion of your paycheck to a money market fund or savings account so that you can build up your emergency savings. You can determine the amount based on reviewing your budget on Mint or any other account aggregation service. Do not overextend yourself, though. Find an amount that is comfortable based on what you are spending now and your sense of where you can easily cut expenses without making major changes in your lifestyle. With automatic transfers to your emergency fund, you won't miss the money coming out of your core paycheck—which is what you'll be using to cover your day-to-day expenses.

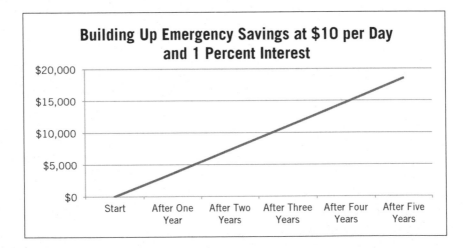

## Getting to Freedom Money—Level 2

Remember the DebtBlaster Strategy in chapter 2? If you have high-interest-rate debt, you can become wealthy much faster by paying it off as soon as possible. This strategy works far better when you set up automatic bill-pay to put any extra dollars you have toward your highest-interest-rate card until that is paid off and then redirect the dollars to the second-highest-interest-rate card. Follow this strategy until you are completely out of debt.

*Important note:* The DebtBlaster Strategy will be successful *only if*

# DebtBlaster Calculator

Making extra payments on your debt is a surefire way to pay it off faster. See how much faster using this DebtBlaster strategy.

### Your Debt Accounts

| Account Name | Current Balance | Interest Rate | Minimum Payment | Lump Sum Payment | Monthly Payments | Months to Pay Off |
|---|---|---|---|---|---|---|
| Credit Card 1 | $7,500 | 19% | $120 | $0 | $220 | 50 |
| Credit Card 2 | $7,500 | 7% | $120 | $0 | $120 | 78 |
| Add Account | | | | | | |

| Total Balance on All Accounts (Total Debt) | $15,000 |
|---|---|

### Additional Contribution Amounts

| New Lump Sum | New Monthly Amount | Total Monthly Payment |
|---|---|---|
| $0 | $100 | $340 |

### DebtBlaster Strategy Estimate

| | Minimum Payments Only | With DebtBlaster Strategy |
|---|---|---|
| Total Years Until Debt Free | 24 years 3 months | 4 years 11 months |
| Total Estimated Cost of Debt | $44,222 | $20,043 |
| Total Estimated Interest | $29,222 | $5,043 |
| Total Interest Saved | | $24,179 |

**Total Months Until Debt Free**

- DebtBlaster Strategy
- Minimum Payments Only

DebtBlaster Strategy: 59
Minimum Payments Only: 291

(months axis: 0, 50, 100, 150, 200, 250, 300, 350)

*you stop charging additional purchases on your credit cards.* Use cash or your debit card so that you don't end up in a vicious cycle of paying down debt only to rack it up again.

You can also sign up for free credit monitoring on sites like credit-karma.com and creditsesame.com, which send you an alert if you miss payments or if someone opens credit in your name. For even stronger protection against identity theft, consider setting a security freeze on your credit reports. This prevents anyone but existing creditors from accessing your credit report without a PIN that you set up.

## Getting to Freedom Money—Level 3

One of the most important steps to building wealth so that you can live life on your own terms is investing as much as you can in your company's retirement plan. One of the advantages of employer-sponsored plans is that the contributions are automatically deducted right from your paycheck. After all, how much would we really save if we had to write a check to our retirement account every month?

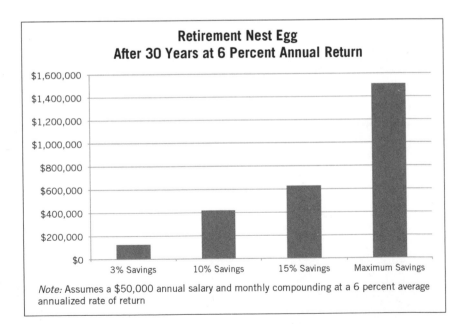

**Retirement Nest Egg After 30 Years at 6 Percent Annual Return**

*Note:* Assumes a $50,000 annual salary and monthly compounding at a 6 percent average annualized rate of return

As the chart demonstrates, the more you save the more wealth you'll have in retirement. The maximum you could have contributed in 2015 was $18,000 if you were under 50, and $24,000 if you were 50 or older. But most people can't save this much all at once, even with the tax deduction, which reduces your net contribution from your paycheck down to around $13,500 (under 50) and $18,000 (over 50) if you are in the 25 percent federal tax bracket.

One solution is auto-escalation. Sign up for this option if your retirement plan offers it and you will see your contribution rate gradually increase automatically over time. You probably won't even notice the difference in your paycheck! The escalation chart shows how much more you will save by putting away an additional 1 percent each year until you reach the maximum.

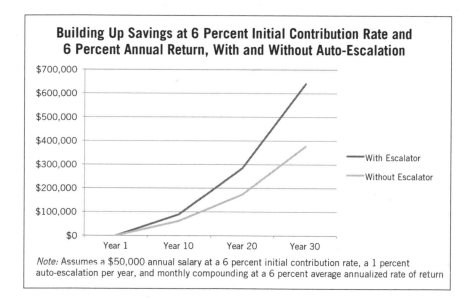

**Building Up Savings at 6 Percent Initial Contribution Rate and 6 Percent Annual Return, With and Without Auto-Escalation**

*Note:* Assumes a $50,000 annual salary at a 6 percent initial contribution rate, a 1 percent auto-escalation per year, and monthly compounding at a 6 percent average annualized rate of return

Your savings aren't the only part of your retirement plan you can automate. You can automate your investments as well. Unless you truly enjoy investing, have the time to research your options and stay on top of managing your portfolio, and have a good track record for doing it yourself, choose an investment option that manages itself for you. Most plans have target date funds that maintain a solid mix of investments to stay diversified and that automatically adjust this mix over time to gradually become more conservative as you get closer to the target retirement date so you're less likely to experience substantial losses in a market downturn just before you retire.

Finally, don't limit your automatic saving to just retirement. You can also automate funding as needed into specific accounts to fund other goals, such as a savings account for a down payment on a home or a 529 savings plan for college. Most 529 plans have age-based investment allocations that work similarly to target date funds.

## WHERE YOU'LL BE FIVE, 10, 15, 20, AND 30 YEARS FROM NOW USING THIS STRATEGY

To illustrate how you can automatically grow wealth by using technology to track and save your money, implement aggressive debt payment plans, and invest for your future, we created the following individual scenario. A 32-year-old man earns $50,000 per year, has $15,000 in credit card debt, $1,000 in checking, and $1,300 in savings, and has access to a company-sponsored retirement plan in which his employer matches his employee contributions dollar for dollar up to 3 percent of his annual compensation. Implementing the Level 1, 2, and 3 strategies just outlined, he can look forward to the following:

### Five Years Later

Debt-free
Fully funded emergency savings fund
Retirement plan balance: $31,630
Saving what he had been paying on his debt for
home purchase
*Total net worth:* $50,080

## Ten Years Later

Still debt-free, with emergency fund
Retirement plan balance: $88,831
Has purchased a home for $250,000 with a down payment
   of $25,000, at a 4 percent interest rate
Has redirected savings for a home to a 529 plan
*Total net worth*: $132,281

## Fifteen Years Later

Still debt-free, with emergency fund
Retirement plan balance: $180,521
$125,680 in home equity
$24,352 in 529 plan
*Total net worth*: $349,003

## Twenty Years Later

Still debt-free, with an emergency fund
Retirement plan balance: $318,732
$245,889 in home equity
$56,941 in 529 plan
*Total net worth*: $640,012

## Thirty Years Later

Still debt-free, with an emergency fund
Mortgage paid off
Retirement plan balance: $805,297
$451,528 in home equity
$158,914 in 529 plan
*Total net worth*: $1,434,189

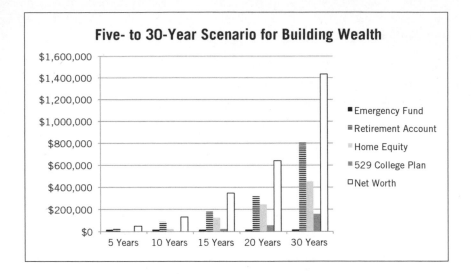

This simple scenario shows how a person with a $50,000 annual salary can reach a net worth of $1.4 million just by setting up some automation and adopting certain habits. You don't have to take big investment risks, invent the next big product, or spend your life in the office to become a millionaire. Moreover, the chart does not account for the *extra* savings generated when you adopt and adhere to a financial identity through techniques that routinize your financial life and create deeply ingrained habits.

Most of the people we have worked with discover that they can save more than they ever imagined when they create a financial lifestyle that works for them, and they end up actually increasing the amount they save and invest over time, which grows their net worth even faster. Something else happens that increases their wealth even more: people who automate their finances to grow their wealth end up applying the same "set yourself up for success" strategy to other aspects of their lives, like their jobs, their health, and their parenting. They use a similar combination of conscious thought about their key goals and values and processes and systems to execute their plans to stay on track without taxing their willpower and giving in to temptations and impulses that could lead them astray.

## HERE'S THE CATCH

Everything I've just shown you looks easy because it's automated, and in that sense it is in fact very easy. You and your partner (if you are in a relationship) can set yourselves up for success in less than a couple of hours simply by creating an automatic savings and investing plan. But there is one important catch—you can't save money that you've already spent. You can set up an automatic monthly payment of $200 to pay off your credit card debt—but if you have spent all the money in your account, that payment will bounce and you'll probably have overdraft charges.

So after you automate your finances, you need to automate yourself! This is something most advisors don't even think about—let alone share with you—since they want to work with you *after* you've reached a certain level of financial success. Advisors don't usually focus on helping people who are still trying to reach that level.

The good news is that this is easier than you might think. It all starts with developing a financial identity.

## THE SIX TYPES OF FINANCIAL IDENTITY

At Financial Finesse, our planners have found that making the automation process personal is an even bigger driver of wealth for clients than automating their finances online. Why? Because by nature we tend to be motivated to stay true to our convictions and, more important, to be accountable to them. You see this when people attach their identity to a specific religious dogma, nutrition plan, or political agenda. Their beliefs are what compel them to act a certain way. And with such consistency comes automation.

Too often people mistakenly believe that choosing a financial identity is about going to one extreme or the other—you're either thrifty or a spendthrift. "She's the spender, I'm the saver," we hear. Or, "He loves to roll the dice. Me, I'm more of a take-my-money-and-run girl." If you think in such black-and-white terms, you'll never have a road map showing you who you are from a financial perspective, how you want to exercise your values through what you purchase (or don't), and how you save, invest, and protect your wealth.

In reality, there are no set "financial styles" that people can ascribe to or groups that they can join to reinforce their values or learn new and better ways to live their financial values. As a result, most people tend to drift. One day (maybe after seeing a major bill), they'll tighten the purse strings but, uh oh, here come the holidays—time to whip out the credit card. People do the same with investing—saving money only sporadically and taking cues from the media or friends, coworkers, and neighbors. Ask anyone whether they prefer rock music or jazz and no doubt you'll get a quick response. Ask them whether they prefer a value or growth investment strategy and you'll probably just get a baffled look.

To fill this "financial identity" void, our team at Financial Finesse has categorized six different financial identities that, by reflecting people's most strongly held values, can be used to drive their financial success. My hope is that one of these financial identities will resonate with you— or perhaps inspire you to create either a hybrid or an entirely new financial identity that will help you define yourself and automate your behaviors for the rest of your life. These identities go far beyond the common question financial advisors ask about whether you consider yourself conservative, moderate, or aggressive.

## Type 1: The Investor

I know this one best, because it happens to be my own financial identity. I don't spend a lot of money on "things" that are going to depreciate in value, like clothes, cars, and electronics. However, I will *invest* in technology because better, faster, and more convenient tech enhances my life enough to merit paying a little more for it. When it comes to kick-around money, I do make an exception for family vacations and romantic trips because I find value in the memories and experiences they create. But, except on rare occasions, I don't pay retail for anything that's going to decline in value if an alternative requires only a little sacrifice or ingenuity (like mixing and matching my wardrobe to keep it fresh), and I hang on to my car until it becomes more expensive to maintain it than to buy a newer one.

It's not that Investors are cheap—they simply put their money in places where they can see it growing, such as real estate, art, collectibles, and antiques.

Because Investors are always aware of what's important to them, decisions to buy come much easier. Because I know this is my financial identity, I can go into a car dealership with a modest car-buying budget, immediately find the car that best suits my needs for that amount, and walk away satisfied. The Investor usually doesn't feel pressured by the expectations or opinions of others and, being more attuned to his or her instincts, generally makes better long-term decisions.

## Type 2: The Bargain Hunter

This is the person who will never, ever pay retail and always manages to find bargain-basement pricing, regardless of how long that takes. My husband is a good Bargain Hunter—he gets immense pleasure from finding and even negotiating a good deal. This makes him my perfect complement: while I'm focusing on the bigger picture of our investments, he comes in and negotiates the cost down.

One thing to watch for if you are a Bargain Hunter—make sure you don't purchase things that you would not otherwise have purchased simply because you can't resist passing up a good deal. The half-priced eBay find may be the deal of the century, but if you don't need it and can't afford it, it would be a ridiculously poor deal to make.

You can avoid this temptation simply by limiting your focus to those things you are going to purchase anyway. Then you make the most of your skills in finding bargains and save tons of money without compromising on quality. The Bargain Hunter really does have an amazing talent—it just needs proper focus.

## Type 3: The Minimalist

Two of my personal heroes, a husband-and-wife team together since their early twenties, fall into this category. They became financially secure in their forties simply by living a simple life and doing what they loved (creating beautiful wooden art pieces). For years they lived in a cabin on an island outside of Seattle, with the bare essentials and only a few modern conveniences. They loved long hikes, camping, singing around the campfire, reading, and getting together with like-minded friends and family who could just hang out and enjoy the beauty that surrounded them on their acres of property. They grew and made their own food and many of their clothes, and they lived the happiest, most fulfilled lives I've ever known two people to have.

If you are someone who loves the simple pleasures of life and feels that material things detract from your enjoyment of it, you are incredibly lucky. Not only are you likely to have a more peaceful and spiritual existence than the rest of us, but you are also more likely to become financially secure early in life and to pursue your passions rather than living for a paycheck. To you it's no sacrifice not to own a big-screen TV (or any TV for that matter), and you couldn't care less what's in fashion at the moment, so on the rare occasions when you're in an expensive store, you can simply marvel at the rest of us buying things we don't really need (sometimes with money we don't actually have). You don't consciously decide not to spend a lot of money on things—it's simply what you do by default because it's part of who you are.

## Type 4: The Planner

This is my late grandmother, who instilled in her grandchildren many of her values about money: every time she went to the store she had a list of everything she wanted to buy and she *refused* to buy anything not on the list. She sometimes took this to an extreme, but at the same time she probably saved hundreds of thousands of dollars in impulse purchases over her lifetime. (She lived to almost 100 and shopped like this from the time she took over the shopping for her family after her mom passed away when she was 15.)

The key to the financial success of those with this financial identity is that, in planning everything in advance, they avoid the sort of impulse purchases the rest of us may be more prone to make.

## Type 5: The Giver

These are the altruistic people who get much more joy from seeing others thrive than they do from improving their own personal situation. They prioritize investments that add real value to the lives of their loved ones and also contribute proportionally more than others do to charity, knowing that this investment will make someone's life much better. For Givers, private school for their children may be a must, especially if the public schools in the area are unexceptional, and they will willingly sacrifice a lot of material comforts to pay the tuition. By the same token, they tend to care very little about their own image and spend only minimal amounts on fashion, jewelry, and cars—the trappings other people find so important.

## Type 6: The Hybrid

It is also possible to have a hybrid financial identity. You may be a Minimalist in most areas but like to splurge on a particular hobby or when buying things for others. Maybe you're a Planner who generally shops from a list but is open to an impulse purchase if it's a great investment or if you can get a really good deal on it. If you're a hybrid, you can define your own identity.

For example, I have a friend who isn't always a Minimalist (he's generally more of an Investor-Planner), but he is a card-carrying Minimalist when it comes to hotels. He grew up very poor but can afford to stay at a nice hotel at this point in his life; still, he feels that nice hotels are a complete waste of money. He stays at the cheapest hotels he can find in safe neighborhoods—no exceptions—and has been doing this for more than 50 years. When my friend travels, he simply finds the best deal, closes his computer, and moves on—while the rest of us go back and forth over whether the nicer hotel is really "worth it."

Ironically, though, he'll drive to the hotel on a long road trip in his gas-guzzling Ferrari. All bets are off for him when it comes to cars—he freely admits to being a spendthrift when it comes to his "toys," which are simply too much fun for him not to spend a significant amount of money on them. I think he'd have to stay in bad hotels every night for three lifetimes to pay for his car habit. The point, though, is this: he knows what he values, and he follows his values with absolute consistency—even with the car habit, which has served him well over the long run.

What's the bottom line? It doesn't matter which identity you have—*as long as you have one.* Why is this so important? When you clearly establish your priorities for how you spend your money—what enriches your life and what detracts from it—you are less likely to overspend and more likely to make true investments that pay off either financially or in the enjoyment they provide to you and your loved ones.

## HOW TO AUTO-THINK

Using technology to implement automation is critically important but overrated, as a computer cannot run your life. Only *you* can live within your means. You can tell a computer to save $100 for your long-term future each month, but if you rack up credit card debt, you'll have to raid that account to pay off your debt. You can tell a computer to direct your investments a certain way, but you can override that decision in a panic if the investment plummets and loses money. You can tell a computer to pay more money each month to your highest-interest-rate credit card, but if you overspend at the same time, you'll end up overdrawn.

It's the *thinking* automatically—habitually—that changes the game. At Financial Finesse, our planners help people live automated lives by leveraging the best technology out there, but more importantly, they first help people automate their thinking—initially by committing to a financial identity and then by identifying bad habits that do not align with it.

Automation begins with your brain, where your decision-making can become like a reflex impervious to temptation or impulse reactions. Sure, you can automate your bank statements via your laptop, but that's no match for what happens when you make your behaviors so automatic that it is almost impossible to sabotage yourself.

In short, becoming an automatic millionaire requires that you change your brain a bit, and especially your perception of your financial life. I think it's a pretty safe bet that you will rarely meet a financial advisor who encourages you to embrace brain plasticity or teaches you the science behind busting bad habits; few advisors would even have you set up an automated bill-pay. Not only is this type of automation not in their wheelhouse, but spending time on it doesn't get them any closer to closing a deal that can help them pay their own bills.

One of our helpline callers, Rebecca, found herself in a predicament that her financial advisor didn't even know about, probably because it wasn't relevant to his business. She was a self-proclaimed shopaholic who tended to run up her credit cards, even in stores where it would seem hard to do that, like chain drugstores. Relocated by her company to a new town, Rebecca was having a hard time finding a social group, so after work she would run an errand to pick up dish soap or something she needed, and an hour and $100 later, she'd walk out of the store with the dish soap and a few bags full of makeup and hair products from the beauty aisle. Rebecca admitted that this kind of shopping somehow eased her loneliness and boredom—she could look forward to going home to her empty apartment because her evening hours would be filled trying out new mud masks and deep oil conditioners. Unfortunately for Rebecca, her spontaneous shopping sprees and frequent spa visits on weekends were costing her hundreds of dollars a month—which she often put on her credit cards.

When you don't have a sense of financial identity, you're subject to your emotions, desires, and impulses, and your actions and reactions become unpredictable, as Rebecca discovered. Unpredictability is the archenemy of consistency.

We had to first work with Rebecca on choosing her financial identity so that she could see how her behaviors were derailing her. Through the previous discussion, I hope you already have more of a sense of your own financial identity, or at least the identity you'd like to have; perhaps you've created a hybrid identity that's just right for you. Now that you've chosen your financial identity, step back and think about your most recent financial actions. Did they include bad habits that you might need to address?

It's human nature to pick up bad habits and negative behaviors. They often provide a rush, a sense of comfort, or even a dulling of our pain that we come to depend on to get through the day. Just within the last few years, scientists have learned a lot more about habits, and one important discovery is that it is almost impossible to give up a bad habit without replacing it with a different, healthier habit.

The idea is to replace not so much the habit itself but the feelings aroused by the habit. If we are forced to give up something we've relied on for a long time, we feel deprived to the point of depression, and that is simply a setup for failure. That's why our planners didn't tell Rebecca to stop looking at beauty products. Instead, they helped her to see that she needed to find a community of like-minded individuals. Instead of cruising the beauty aisle, she began to go on Pinterest or look for Groupons to spas, and she invited a coworker out for a lunchtime mani-pedi.

Habitual actions usually have very little to do with the actions themselves and a great deal to do with the reason behind the actions. Remember that we are all prone to unhealthy habits and behaviors because they give us a temporary "fix" that makes life more fun, more exciting, or, in some cases, more bearable. Examining the reasons for your habits will certainly help you get better at creating positive replacement habits that accomplish the same thing, only better. And there's another reason for replacing a bad habit with a good habit: if you don't, you're much more likely to fall back into the bad habit!

Now it's time to brainstorm ideas for how you can take actions and make decisions that are *consistent* with your identity and your goals—in other words, how you can form habits that foster and develop your financial identity.

As you consider your habits alongside your financial identity in order to align them, take the opportunity to identify what usually derails you financially. Are you a compulsive shopper like Rebecca? According to our data, shopping—especially for particular items, such as electronics, shoes, and cars, which kick logic out the window for aficionados—is the biggest culprit in financial distress. But there are other ways to get financially derailed, including investing emotionally, taking big financial risks for the excitement of it, or taking on too much debt to invest in your future in the assumption that you'll strike it rich and pay it off.

In almost all cases, people are aware of the bad habits that are sabotaging their financial lives. Even so, they don't usually share this critical information with their financial advisors. In the rare instance that anyone thinks to share such history, an advisor is likely to simply tell them to stop doing whatever it is they're doing, just as a doctor would tell a heart patient to quit smoking. Knowing what we know, though, we can see how counterproductive such advice could be.

If we were to tell Rebecca and the thousands of other shopaholics we counsel to quit their senseless spending cold turkey, they would likely all fail—as almost always happens when *anyone* quits *anything* cold turkey. Whatever shopaholics are trying to achieve through their sprees would go unfulfilled, and they would end up feeling even worse, having been offered no coping mechanism—that is, a good habit—to use to find the satisfaction they're looking for.

What our planners do instead is brainstorm with clients to find some healthier habits to replace their negative habits, as they did with Rebecca. For example, the temporary solace that shoppers feel during a spree can be replaced with couponing, joining investment clubs, and even becoming a product reviewer or secret shopper for a fee. These are all great habit replacements that can rewire the brains of automatic spenders and turn them into automatic savers.

Once you identify your bad habits, determine which ones you'll make a commitment to breaking and devise a replacement habit that is healthier. You may find, as Carly did, that sometimes a replacement habit can be life-changing.

Carly was generally good with money but loved to buy shoes, and her inability to stop buying shoes was compromising her ability to become financially secure enough to quit her job to start her own business. Like so many others, she was aware of her problem, but couldn't seem to kick it. When she called our financial helpline, she was at her wit's end. Even though she had done a relatively good job of saving money, she wasn't where she wanted to be—and it honestly all came down to shoes!

The planner who worked with Carly helped her identify what it was about shoes that she liked so much. It turned out that it was the thrill of finding something beautiful and pairing it with other outfits in her closet. She loved fashion and found delight in how a simple shoe could completely transform a look. She also enjoyed the reactions of others when she wore her ensembles. Carly had impeccable taste (she even gave us a video tour of her closet, and it was a marvel), and virtually everyone commented on her ability to find just the right outfit, with just the right shoe, for the occasion. Her fashion sense was one of the things she loved most about herself, so cutting her budget for shoes was like cutting out a part of her identity—which was precisely why it was so hard for her to kick her habit.

As Carly and our planner talked, they began to think of ways Carly could get the same feeling of satisfaction and accomplishment without actually purchasing shoes. Together, they discussed different ideas and scenarios, and finally they landed on something that helped not only kick Carly's shoe habit but also generate an extra $25,000 in income. Carly became a fashion consultant in her free time, and one service she provided was closet makeovers for friends and acquaintances. Sharing her talents with others and seeing their excitement and pride when she found the perfect outfits for them and turned their closets from drab to chic, Carly felt more fulfilled than ever—and became wealthier in the process!

## HOW TO MAKE YOUR GOOD HABIT STICK

Let's say you've targeted your bad habit and found a suitable replacement action that you feel is aligned with the goals of your financial identity. How do you make it automatic? In other words, how do you make it a habit?

Let's face it, the bad habit you are shedding didn't just happen overnight—it developed over time. The same holds true for your good habit, but there are a few things you should know and can do that will ensure that it sticks. Remember, we want your good habit to reinforce your financial identity. As your new good habit takes hold, your identity will be strengthened and will reinforce, in turn, your good habit, and a new positive cycle will ensue. The process of habit identification and formation is not over, however, once you've replaced a bad habit with a good one. To align a good habit with your financial identity and make it stick you have to build on that habit.

Depending on the study, the researcher, and the era when the study was published, you'll find variations in how long experts believe it takes to form a habit. Back in the 1950s, it was famously said to take 21 days to form a habit. New research, however, says 66 days is more like it. However long it takes is irrelevant, since each person is so different. The important takeaway from research on habit formation is that a new action must be done as consciously and consistently as possible (don't worry, you can screw up occasionally) in order to become automatic.

I keep this in mind every time I have to nag my five-year-old to brush his teeth. Sure, I know that his baby teeth are just "practice" teeth, and that until his permanent teeth come in, it's not the end of the world if he falls asleep without flossing. In nagging him, however, I'm trying to instill an automatic behavior that will be so habitual that he'll reap the rewards later and avoid periodontal disease at the age of 35.

Not all habits are created equal. Some might be easier to break, and others might be more easily replaced. That's why it takes two actions—a one-two punch—to make sure a good habit sticks. The first is routinizing, and the second is premeditation.

## Make It Routine

The first way to build a habit is to make it a routine that you follow consistently and that eventually becomes automatic to you, so that you don't have to actively think about it. The new habit becomes just "what you do," and not doing it makes you uncomfortable. Later in the chapter, I'll share some exciting ways to routinize your finances using technology, but here it's important to note that sometimes technology only provides an assist.

For example, let's say you've reserved the biweekly date and time of Sunday at 5:00 P.M. to sit down with yourself (or your partner) to review your finances. The alert on your phone can tell you it's time, but is it in your routine to stop whatever else you're doing, sit down, and actually review your finances? You have to be accountable to yourself and consciously decide to follow through when the prompt you've set up goes off. Almost any new habit is like going to the gym: the worst part is getting there, but once you're in the zone you're so happy you did it.

After you do sit down, let's say you review your savings account and discover that it's getting low because you've been celebrating your birthday with various friends and family for the past couple of weeks. Your partner also mentions that the roof is leaking a little bit in the spare bedroom/home office. Because you're carrying through on your routine financial review, you become aware of these two situations and can take action to minimize their costs. You deal with the birthday-related expenses by getting back on track with your budget, even finding a few more expenses to cut in the process. And even though your emergency savings fund is fully funded, you decide to reinstate an automatic transfer of 5 percent of your paycheck to the account just in case the roof problem turns out to be more expensive than you think. Last, you meet with the highest-rated roofer you can find, and he tells you that he can fix the leak with work that will put off the need to redo the roof for at least 10 more years. Sure enough, there's a higher cost to this fix than you'd anticipated, but you'll be able to save thousands of dollars by catching the leak early and going to the best roofer in town to handle the problem before it becomes a full-on emergency. You've also just learned that you'll need to purchase a new roof in 10 years, so you can plan for this expense without getting caught off guard.

After you begin reaping so many benefits from simply sticking to your weekly routine of sitting down for a financial review, you'll probably see the tangible value in this action and keep doing it—thereby making it a habit. When you get to the point where missing a financial review at your kitchen table makes you feel like something's off and you need to take care of it right away, that's automation!

*Three Routines You Can Start Right Now*
The following are routines that all of us at Financial Finesse personally follow and recommend to everyone we work with. They're so easy that you won't even have to leave your chair to get them started.

**1. Meet for regular financial reviews.** Being faithful to the routine of a biweekly meeting with yourself or a partner keeps you honest, accountable, transparent, and apprised of situations large and small. This is an opportunity to review how you are spending your money and to make adjustments, but more important, you can establish and review your progress toward key financial goals. If you have a partner, this review ensures that you are working together to continually build your wealth rather than operating off of separate priorities and spending habits.

We always recommend having a meeting with yourself as the first step in implementing a routine. It requires little effort and will keep you on track to have sufficient savings for emergencies while mitigating other costs that otherwise could get out of control. A routine meeting also allows you to stay on track with your automated plans so that you can make sure that automatic transfers from your paycheck aren't putting you in an overdraft situation and back in debt.

Lastly, a routine meeting is an excellent way to ensure that you are on track with your financial goals. If the market has been tougher than you expected, you may decide that you have to save more. Or maybe the market has been excellent and you've ended up with a financial windfall. Such a windfall and others, like an inheritance or a significant promotion, might allow you to upgrade your lifestyle and set new future goals. Maybe it's now possible to pay for an Ivy League education for your children, or to retire five to 10 years early. Maybe your partner could now "go for the dream" rather than stay in a passionless job.

The bottom line is that financial situations change every single day, and new challenges and opportunities are constantly presenting themselves. Automation is great but useless without a routine financial review that alerts you to where you can adjust your money management and financial goals to fully maximize your wealth.

**2. Aggregate your accounts.** People commonly have several types of accounts at different financial institutions. To make your biweekly meetings much easier and more effective, aggregate your accounts using an aggregation service, such as mint.com, and add checking it to your daily routine. Simply using one financial institution for all your banking can be a good substitute for an account aggregation service.

In making a habit of checking your accounts every day, you're looking for unusual transactions that may be fraudulent and ensuring that all your account balances are in line with your expectations. If you make this a daily routine (which is far less time than many people spend on their Facebook or Instagram accounts), you'll begin to get a good grip on your financial situation, and that will automatically affect how you manage your money. For instance, when you discover that you've got just $200 in your bank account until your next paycheck in two days, you'll avoid any unnecessary expenses so as not to become overdrawn or tempted to take money out of your emergency fund for nonessential expenses.

**3. Make *how* you organize your finances a habit.** Once you've made a habit of organizing your finances, stick to it the same way you stick to showering, brushing your teeth, and eating dinner every night. Routines become easy when there are systems in place. The key here is setting up a system that works. If you are naturally organized and have fun thinking of creative ways to get organized, you'll probably skip this section. I've known people who scan receipts once a month and save them on their hard drive or in cloud-based storage they can access online. That's too much for me. I save receipts in a baggie that I keep in my bottom desk drawer, along with all my important documents (which I also make sure I keep electronic copies of—they are too important to *not* store electronically). Don't forget to tell friends and family where these documents are located, in the event that something happens to you.

## Premeditation

As mentioned earlier, habit formation requires a one-two punch—routinizing a new behavior in conjunction with premeditation. Premeditation, or predetermining your decisions, really is where the rubber meets the road when it comes to sticking to a habit.

Through premeditation, instead of resisting temptation each time you encounter something, you commit to a certain choice beforehand in order to avoid being derailed or relapsing. I have friends who predetermine their food choices by looking up menus online so that they don't derail their healthy eating resolutions once they're at the restaurant. I know other people who resolve not to spend money on paraphernalia at concerts, pro sports games, or the circus and back up that resolve by leaving their credit cards at home. It works like a charm.

I started predetermining my choices when I saw where I was wasting my money:

- Buying books and magazines—I'm completely addicted to reading.
- Dining out at restaurants—some are more expensive than others, but I like them all equally.
- Purchasing highly rated wine—I thought it would taste better and never considered finding wines I like that are more affordable.

Then here's what I did:

- I decided not to buy hardcover books or magazines unless I'm in the airport, where I somehow find the experience to be calming (I'm a nervous flyer). Now, outside of airport splurges—but limiting myself to three magazines—I borrow free ebooks from Amazon Prime or purchase online editions, which are considerably cheaper. By the way, this decision is much more in line with my financial identity (the Investor), as the magazines and books are not likely to increase in value over time.
- I decided to limit dining out to special occasions.
- I decided not to drink when I go out unless the restaurant offers a wine I like that's less than a certain cost per glass.

These minor choices save me more than $150 per month, which at an 8 percent return translates into over $27,000 within 10 years—enough to pay for my son's first year of college. (That is, if he goes to a state school close to home like he's supposed to!) All kidding aside, it is amazing how small changes like these add up. As a bonus, I've lost about 10 pounds, mostly from eating out less but also from drinking less wine. I look better, I feel better, and my finances are in better shape. And because I premeditated about all these decisions to make sure they align with and reinforce my financial identity, I don't have to actively resist temptation. I have learned to "auto-think" situations, an approach that takes all the unpredictability and impulsivity out of the equation.

To be successful in deciding ahead of time what you will cut out of your spending, I recommend taking baby steps. Don't try to implement more than five cuts at a time. Talk about major deprivation mode! Plus, it's harder to keep track of too many cuts, and trying to do it will slow you down. You'll be more successful if you really focus on just a few cuts.

Once you automate all you can, you'll begin facing decisions around how to grow your wealth in accounts outside of work, and how to protect the nest egg you've built. That's where an advisor comes into play. In the next chapter, we'll discuss how to select a financial advisor who is an ideal fit for your specific financial needs.

# 8

## How to Find the Right Advisor for You

**I was sitting** across the table from the head of player development for a major sports association, and he asked me what percentage of financial advisors commit fraud with their clients' accounts.

The answer might surprise you—it certainly did him. The number of advisors who are truly bogus—who are committing criminal activities like running Ponzi schemes—is a mere fraction of 1 percent, and that percentage is even lower among financial advisors with strong credentials they could not have acquired without adhering to a strict fiduciary standard.

The sports executive was shocked. His guess had been 40 percent, based on the amount of money stolen from professional athletes, who are obviously high-profile targets. But the vast majority of advisors working even with this population are in fact doing the right thing. Unfortunately, the advisor who's had a 40-year career helping hundreds of people become financially secure and independent is not the stuff of a headline news story. But it should be reassuring to know that most financial advisors are trustworthy souls.

Every so often, however, a scandalous story does make the headlines about an advisor who's swindled a client out of a lot of money. As a result, far too many people, afraid of becoming victims themselves, then decide not to use an advisor. This is the same kind of thinking behind keeping your money under a mattress because you're worried your bank might fail. The reality is that you are many times more vulnerable to losing your money stuffed under a mattress to a fire, a burglar, or even a desperate family member who regularly "borrows" from your stash (with or without your knowledge) with every intention of paying it back but never does. In addition, by squirreling money away at home, you're guaranteed to lose money over time owing to inflation, which is typically offset by the interest rates paid by money market funds, CDs, and even regular savings accounts. So, in an effort to "protect" yourself, you do the opposite—you put yourself at much higher risk.

Also putting themselves at higher risk are people who don't use an advisor when they really need one. These people overwhelmingly end up underinsured, poorly diversified, and faced with tax bills that are significantly higher than they might otherwise be. A small minority of people who accumulate the beginnings of a nest egg *can* manage it themselves, but they must have three key ingredients:

**1.** Knowledge
**2.** Time
**3.** An ability to react rationally to changes in their financial situation and to maintain a prudent course of action rather than an emotional one

I am independent by nature, and I'd like to believe I'm knowledgeable about financial planning, but I still have a financial advisor—mostly because I lack both time and an ability to emotionally distance myself from the ups and downs of the market. Think about it—I run a company that helps people properly invest and protect their assets *every single* day. It is my life's passion, but it doesn't prevent me from being tempted to sell my own investments when the market plummets, to choose mutual funds that have had great performance (right when they are at their most overvalued), or to avoid facing my own mortality and the likelihood that I will end my life in a nursing home. I need an advisor precisely because I care too much about my own money and would probably give in to my emotions if I didn't have someone more removed from my situation who can keep me in check when I start to get worried, feel greedy, or procrastinate about important decisions.

I devoted chapter 3 first and foremost to bogus advisors who are criminals for two reasons:

**1. Bogus advisors, though they represent a very small percentage of the financial advisor community, can completely wipe you out financially.** I want to save as many people as possible from the fate of doing all the right things to build their nest egg and then losing it when they decide to invest their money with a criminal who is actually stealing it. I know people who were personally affected by Bernie Madoff's Ponzi scheme, and I saw what that did to their lives. They didn't just lose money — they were deeply violated psychologically, and the emotional trauma lives on even among those who have recovered financially. No one should ever have to go through that.

**2. Equally important, "bad apples" need to be exposed and weeded out of what is actually a very noble profession.** Bogus advisors should be exposed not just because of the havoc they wreak, but also because they *discourage* people from using a legitimate advisor who could help them grow and protect their wealth.

This book, and especially this chapter, is about taking control of your own money because no one is more affected by what happens to it than you and your loved ones, and also because all of us can become financially secure if we make the right choices with our money. Part of taking control is knowing when you need help and how to find the right person to help you. You wouldn't attempt to take out your child's appendix, for instance, even though you care more about his or her life than the doctor performing the surgery does. The point is, whenever you're a guardian — of money, of a business or nonprofit, of children or elderly parents, or even of a sports team or classroom—you need to know:

1. When you need help
2. What type of help you need
3. How to find the best possible help based on the situation at hand

This chapter will help you address these issues and find an advisor who will help you grow and protect your wealth. This person will also help you avoid some of the most common mistakes almost all of us make when left to our own devices—the same way my advisors have helped me do the right thing when I needed an outside perspective unswayed by emotion.

## WHEN DO YOU NEED AN ADVISOR?

Unfortunately, you might think you need an advisor when you actually don't. If you have financial problems or are only beginning to save and invest your money, a financial advisor can't help you all that much; instead, you should take advantage of the resources available at work—the employee assistance programs and financial wellness programs mentioned in chapter 1. Or, if you are unemployed, there may be nonprofit organizations in your community that could help you get back on your feet.

Advisors, like bankers, want to work with people who already have money. They typically are compensated based on how much you invest in various financial products, services, and mutual funds, so the more money you have, the more attractive you are as a client.

It's time to consider hiring an advisor when you are feeling financially comfortable but want to make sure your savings are invested and protected appropriately so that you can go from being financially comfortable to financially secure and independent. This is precisely what many people miss: they think they are doing fine taking care of their finances by themselves, until they make a mistake and end up back at square one because they did not hire a qualified advisor to help them. Remember the statistic I first cited in chapter 4: *people who go it alone end up with a return 3 percent lower per year, on average, than those who use an advisor*—and this doesn't factor in those who end up uninsured in the face of a catastrophe.

You probably need a financial advisor if:

- You have money to invest and you have maxed out what you are eligible to contribute monetarily to your retirement plans and other employee benefits, you have paid down all your high-interest-rate debt, and you have set up an emergency fund.
- You are in a position to regularly commit money on a monthly or annual basis to fund your key financial goals and now need help determining the right financial planning and investing strategy for these goals.
- You have wealth (either slowly built or suddenly acquired) and want to make sure you protect it through proper diversification, tax planning, and insurance strategies.
- You are ready to retire or are in retirement and want to make sure you don't outlive your money. For example, a good financial advisor can help you annuitize a portion of your retirement assets, converting some of your nest egg into a monthly stream of income to last the rest of your life. An advisor can also help with adjusting your investment and distribution strategies as you age to maintain your financial security and with estate planning so that your heirs receive your assets in a tax-efficient way.
- You want to buy certain financial products or services, like insurance, annuities, or mutual funds, and you want to work with someone you trust to make wise decisions about which types of investments are best for your situation. The operative word here is "trust"—selecting and managing a trusted advisor who has your best interest in mind can be as invaluable as a bogus advisor is dangerous.

## The Cost of Not Hiring a Financial Planner When You Need One

For every dollar lost to bogus advisors, probably $100 is lost when people *don't* hire an advisor when they truly need to do so. This cost is hard to calculate because it's hypothetical, but at Financial Finesse we see it in some form or fashion every single day. We regularly hear variations on the following stories:

**1.** A widow's husband died without life insurance and with debts she didn't know about. Would an advisor have changed this situation? Well, a competent one would have identified the need for life insurance for a single-income household, especially one without significant savings set aside.

**2.** A 24-year-old woman received an inheritance of over $500,000 in a traditional IRA when her dad died. Invested at an 8 percent rate of return — which would have been reasonable to expect for an aggressive portfolio appropriate for her needs — that money could have continued to grow, tax-deferred, and become a retirement nest egg of over $2.5 million by the time she was 45, and $5 million by the time she was 54. Instead, she cashed it all out, paid a heavy tax bill, quit her job, and spent down what was left in just five years. At 29, she was penniless and trying to rebuild her once-promising career in advertising, starting from the bottom all over again. A competent financial advisor would have told her about the tax consequences of taking money out of the IRA, showed her how much she could earn over time by investing the money, and warned her that she could quickly drain the account by choosing to live a lavish lifestyle for a few short years. This young woman did not, however, seek financial help — and neither did her father, who actually forgot she was the beneficiary of the account! A competent financial advisor would have warned him of the risks associated with acquiring a lot of money as a young adult and probably would have talked him into establishing a trust in her name to delay or divide the distribution of the assets so as to protect her financial future.

**3.** A man retired at 76 after a successful career as an entrepreneur who cherished his independence and eschewed all offers for financial advice. He was diagnosed with Alzheimer's two years into retirement, with no plan for the distribution of his assets or his long-term care, and the inability to manage either of these things himself.

## WHAT TYPE OF ADVISOR DO YOU NEED?

Legally, anyone can claim he or she is a "financial advisor" and start a business doling out financial advice. If an advisor sells financial products and services, there are some requirements, but they are extremely light. Virtually every other professional trade that can have a significant impact on people's lives, safety, and peace of mind requires rigorous training, but all financial advisors have to do in order to sell mutual funds and variable contracts is pass a background check and roughly three hours' worth of exam questions. Even cosmetologists need more training!

This becomes a major issue for you in looking for the right advisor because it can be difficult to sift through an advisor's credentials without knowing what to look for or how to confirm that your advisor really has the training and experience required to grow and protect your wealth.

Another reality is that those employed in the personal advising field range from brokers who only sell investments, to advisors who focus on a single area such as business planning, tax planning, or estate planning, to those who focus on specific segments of the population, such as retirees, executives, or professional athletes. I could go through all these different types of advisors, but that's a book unto itself and, even to me, not a very interesting one. So let me try to cut through the clutter.

Well over 90 percent of the people who need a financial advisor need someone who will work with them based on their specific goals, using solid principles of financial planning that are proven to grow and sustain wealth over time. They do *not* need a broker who specializes in selling specific stocks to individuals based on what his or her company recommends, nor do they need a money manager who has full discretion to manage all of their money—without consulting them first.

A true financial planner does not simply sell you financial products or services and then walk away. You should have an advisor who approaches your situation with your best interest in mind and works with you holistically to address your needs and goals on an ongoing basis. This person will operate as your partner, actively looking out for your needs and working closely with you to create an appropriate investment portfolio based on your goals as well as a strategy to minimize your taxes and protect your assets from loss through insurance and estate planning strategies.

Unless your situation is unique, you are probably best off with a generalist—such as a personal financial planner, a financial professional akin to a primary care physician. The most rigorous and broad-based financial planning designation in the industry is the CFP® designation, which requires a bachelor's degree and completion of a university-level education program certified by the CFP® Board of Standards, three years of experience, passing a six-hour, two-day financial planning exam, 30 hours of mandatory continuing education per year, and a commitment to uphold a fiduciary standard—which means putting clients' interests above one's own. These requirements ensure that a CFP® has been educated in every major area of financial planning and is specifically taught to work with clients on a personal level based on the clients' needs and goals.

This doesn't mean that any CERTIFIED FINANCIAL PLANNER™ professional is by default a good choice for you, that all CFPs® are guaranteed to be up to speed on all the ins and outs of financial planning, or that you should automatically rule out planners who don't have a CFP® designation. A CFP® designation is simply a good place to start if you want to find a planner who—at least on paper—has the skills, expertise, and approach to create a financial plan and investment strategy specifically focused on your needs.

A good advisor, like a good primary care physician, works with specialists when needed. You may have issues that require legal advice or extensive accounting or tax planning expertise, or perhaps you're looking for someone with knowledge about unusual or "alternative" investments. Nevertheless, it is critical to be able to turn to that one key person you have screened, are properly managing, and are confident "has your back."

## When Do You Need to Find a Specialist?

As noted, sometimes you may need to consider a specialist or a different model. About 10 percent of the people we work with who need an advisor also need either a specialist to supplement the services provided by a more general financial planner or a specialist to replace the planner's services. They fall mainly into three categories:

1. People who have complicated tax situations
2. People who need legal help—typically to set up a will or trust in order to pass assets to their heirs
3. People who suddenly become wealthy through their own efforts or through an unexpected windfall

*Complicated Tax Situations*
If you have complex tax planning issues, you may need to consult a tax professional like an Enrolled Agent (EA) or a Certified Public Accountant (CPA) who specializes in individual income taxes. You may need help not only with tax planning but also with tax preparation, since you may be subject to obscure tax laws (or eligible for loopholes) that neither your planner nor standard tax preparation services will catch. If you have a complicated tax situation, it is critical that your tax professional and financial planner collaborate because your tax situation is likely to have implications for how and where you invest your money and how and when you take distributions from different accounts.

A tax professional may be important if you are in any of the following situations:

- You own a small business with an S-corp or LLC structure that makes you personally liable for taxes on the business's gains and losses.
- You are an expatriate and need to resolve how to handle US taxes along with foreign taxes.
- You have a job in which you must pay taxes in multiple states.
- You have highly volatile income or investments (e.g., a large amount of your wealth is in company stock options, you regularly buy and sell real estate, or your income varies a lot from year to year), and you need to be very careful not to end up owing more in taxes than you can afford to pay.
- You are a high-net-worth investor with a broad array of different investments, many of them complex in nature (like hedge funds, limited partnerships, or private equity).

## The Cost of *Not* Hiring a Tax Professional If You Need One

We work regularly with young executives who have climbed the corporate ladder so quickly that they don't fully comprehend the fact that they are wealthy and that filing their tax returns themselves via the usual 11th-hour race to the post office could cost them a fortune—or worse, put them and their families at risk for a nasty IRS audit. We see this a lot with young doctors, attorneys, and consultants who make hundreds of thousands or millions of dollars per year when they are only a decade or so out of graduate school. They remember living the starving student lifestyle like it was yesterday and continue living it to some extent, even as their houses and cars get bigger. For many of them, the concept of hiring an expensive CPA or estate planning attorney seems ridiculous when just a few years before they had virtually no income, were up to their ears in debt, and were sleeping on a futon.

Here's an example from the thousands we've worked with—just one of the millions of Americans each year who don't get the tax planning advice they need.

Jeremy was in his midforties when he switched jobs and needed to decide what to do with his $50,000 401(k) from his previous employer. A buddy of his urged him to roll his 401(k) into a Roth IRA, since he was young and would have the advantage of many years of tax-free growth going forward. What Jeremy missed as part of that conversation was the tax bill associated with the rollover.

When Jeremy did his taxes several months later, he found that he had a balance due of over $4,000. Not having the money available, he had to ask for a partial withdrawal from his Roth IRA, which cost him an additional $25,000 in penalties the following tax year. Bottom line: had Jeremy consulted a tax professional at the beginning, that person probably would have made sure Jeremy had the extra outside funds to handle the conversion tax before rolling his 401(k) into a Roth IRA.

### When You Need an Attorney

While low-cost or even free online services may be sufficient for simple estate planning documents, such as an advance health care directive and durable power of attorney, you'll probably want to hire a qualified estate planning attorney to draft more complex legal documents like wills and trusts.

Unless you're a single individual with no children and little property, your estate is probably more complicated than it may seem. The problem is that it takes only one mistake to completely void all of your wishes.

Linda recently remarried, and because her new husband had children of his own, she decided to draft a will to make sure her own children from her previous marriage would inherit some of her property. To save money she drafted the will online, but she made sure it was properly filled out and executed, including having it signed by two witnesses. Many years later, Linda's husband died, and then Linda did too.

Although Linda had taken the proper precautions with her will, she didn't realize that her state required that witnesses testify that the will was properly executed. Since her original two witnesses were now deceased as well and couldn't testify, her husband's children were able to contest the will. After several expensive and emotionally trying years in probate court, they cut Linda's children out of their inheritance and left them with nothing.

Had Linda consulted an estate planning attorney, that person would have told her that she could have her witnesses testify in advance through an affidavit. If she had done so, her children would have avoided this entire legal nightmare.

### Sudden Wealth

If you suddenly become wealthy, whether through your own efforts or through an unexpected windfall (inheritance, lottery, exceptional real estate investment, employee stock options that surge in value), you may need to consult the kind of specialist who can be found in the private client services department of a major financial institution. You could even find yourself with millions of dollars to invest if you do an excellent job of saving and investing—especially if you have a very generous corporate retirement plan to which your employer contributes funds.

Private client services departments are set up to cater to wealthy individuals (usually with $1 million or more to invest), who typically have more complex financial situations. They often provide favorable fees, access to alternative investments that may make sense if your situation is more complex, and concierge-level service that provides someone at the ready any time you need help with a financial transaction.

Another option is to set up what is called a "family office" with financial professionals you hire on salary. They oversee all of your investments and tax planning, from real estate to international investing to complex hedging strategies that reduce your exposure to economic and market risks. Family offices very often manage clients' expenses, distributions, tax filings, charitable donations, and trust funds set up for loved ones. This arrangement is obviously expensive and appropriate only if you end up with a very large nest egg, but it's an important option to consider if this is your situation. A family office provides *full* support around all aspects of your finances, with no conflicts of interest. That is virtually impossible to find among even the best independent financial planners, who focus on investing but typically don't get involved with real estate or the day-to-day management of clients' income and expenses.

## WHERE DO YOU FIND AN ADVISOR?

Once you figure out what kind of advisor you need, the next step is to find advisors in your area whom you can interview. We recommend that you interview at least three advisors who are qualified, on paper, to meet your needs.

The following chart outlines the resources you can use to find advisors:

| Advisor | Resources |
|---|---|
| Financial planner (generalist) | CERTIFIED FINANCIAL PLANNER™ (CFP®) Board: letsmakeaplan.org |
| | National Association of Personal Financial Advisors (NAPFA) (fee-only advisors): napfa.org |
| | Garrett Planning Network (fee-only advisors who charge an hourly rate): garrettplanningnetwork.com |
| | Alliance of Comprehensive Planners (ACP) (fee-only advisors who charge an annual retainer and prepare taxes): acplanners.org |
| Tax professional | National Association of Enrolled Agents (NAEA): naea.org |
| | Your state society of CPAs |
| Estate planning attorney | American Academy of Estate Planning Attorneys: aaepa.com |
| | National Network of Estate Planning Attorneys: nnepa.com |

*A cautionary note:* Many people ask friends and family to recommend an advisor. This can be dangerous, as many people judge the quality of their advisors by their short-term investment performance, which is not a reliable indicator of how well that advisor will manage your money over the long term. In fact, high short-term returns can be a red flag for fraud, overly risky investments, or investments that have become overvalued and are due for a correction.

## HOW DO YOU SELECT THE RIGHT ADVISOR?

So let's assume that you have found three advisors who appear to meet your needs based on the research you did. How do you narrow it down and make your final pick? Here are some questions we recommend that you ask when interviewing prospective advisors:

**1. "What services do you provide?"** Just because an advisor has the proper credentials doesn't mean that he or she will provide the type of financial services you're looking for. Are you looking for someone who sells financial products, someone who will manage your money, or someone who will just provide financial advice? Are you looking for comprehensive financial planning or just help with investments? Are you looking for help with tax preparation, or do you also need help with tax planning?

**2. "How do you charge?"** Make sure you have a full understanding of all the costs involved and the conflicts of interest they may present. The advisor should be very clear and direct and willing to spell out exactly what the costs might be over the long run. You do not want to be surprised when it comes to the advisor's charges, so if the response to this question is too vague, it could be a deal-breaker.

Tax professionals and estate planning attorneys tend to charge by the hour for the service provided, but financial advisors can be compensated in a multitude of ways. Because some collect a commission on the products they sell, they can be biased toward selling high-fee investments or, at the very least, avoid recommending certain financial products that might be better for you but aren't ones they sell.

If you want to avoid hiring an advisor on a commission basis, you may prefer to work with a "fee-only" advisor instead. Not all fee-only advisors are compensated the same way, however. Some work on an hourly fee or annual retainer basis, while others charge a percentage of the assets they manage for you, typically around 1 percent a year. That number may look small, but when you do the math, that's $5,000 a year on a $500,000 portfolio. They also tend to require a minimum amount of assets to manage, so you may not qualify. Fee-only advisors may not be biased toward certain investments, but they can still be inclined to encourage you to invest all you can with them rather than doing something else with your money, such as paying down debt or purchasing a rental property. These kinds of moves may provide little benefit for the financial advisor.

Some advisors may hold themselves out as "fee-based" advisors. These advisors may charge an asset-based fee and/or collect commissions. This is why it's so important to get total clarification about an advisor's compensation up-front.

Perhaps the cleanest and usually least expensive way to compensate a financial advisor is the same way we often compensate other professionals: *by paying an hourly fee, flat rate, or annual retainer.* Unfortunately, these advisors can be harder to find. I have included some organizations in the chart on page 174 that can help you find them. Please be sure to go back and review those possibilities.

**3. "Who will I be working with?"** You may be meeting with a "star" advisor only to discover that you'll be assigned later to a more junior advisor. Some advisors also work in teams, in which case you'll probably want to meet everyone on the team. This is another area where you don't want surprises.

**4. "What's your investment philosophy?"** If your advisor will be helping you with investments, you'll want to be comfortable with his or her approach. Does your advisor take discretionary control over your account? If so, your advisor can trade quickly to take advantage of market opportunities, since your prior approval isn't required, but you give up control, including over trading costs. What type of investments does your advisor recommend? Just stocks and bonds or alternative investments too? Alternative investments can add diversification to your portfolio but can also be risky and quite expensive, so they may not be worth it. Does your advisor use an active, passive, or mixed strategy? An active strategy gives you the opportunity to outperform the markets, while a passive strategy is the cheapest and tends to produce the best long-term returns. How customized will your portfolio be? Will your advisor take taxes and your outside investments into account?

**5. "Do you have clients like me you can provide as references?"** You want to treat your search for an advisor like any job interview. Asking for clients who are similar to you could force an advisor out of using the regular "go-to" positive references, and your discussion with similar clients is likely to be more relevant to you.

Keep in mind that you are not looking for the best of three advisors; rather, you are looking for the advisor who is right for you. If you aren't fully comfortable with any of the three you interview, interview three more. Remember, this is *your* money for life, and this is not a decision to take lightly. Often, our intuition is stronger than we realize—if it doesn't feel right, it's probably not.

The advisor you select in the end should not only meet all your criteria but also be someone with whom you feel a real personal connection. People who don't like their advisors are less likely to meet with them regularly, and communication can become a major issue over time.

You aren't looking for a money wizard who can get better returns than any other advisor. Money wizards are a myth. The way to grow wealth over the long term is through a diligent investment strategy that is low-cost, tax-efficient, and in line with your goals and risk tolerance. There is no magic to it, so if you don't like the advisor—well, don't hire the advisor.

## HOW SHOULD YOU MANAGE YOUR ADVISOR?

It's not enough to select the right advisor. Even the best advisors are human and prone to mistakes or misunderstandings if not properly managed. Remember the analogy I used in chapter 2 about managing your money like you're running a business and making decisions in that vein? The same line of thinking applies to managing your financial planner.

As a business owner, I believe my corporate attorney is the best of the best, and I couldn't be more grateful for all the ways he's helped me over the years. He has saved our firm far more than he has charged us by helping us put the right agreements and processes in place to protect ourselves appropriately. However, I can never lose sight of the fact that Financial Finesse is not his business. It is mine.

As invested as our corporate attorney is in helping us, he doesn't care as much as I do about the future of the company; nor does he know all of our strategic plans, our challenges, or even the business concerns and issues of each partnership we establish—that is, not until I communicate these to him so that he can ensure that my goals as a business owner are met. Even then, I review every single document to make sure I understand it, and I ask for clarity on what I don't understand. Usually when I don't understand something it's because his legal expertise is greater than mine and what he's recommending is needed. But sometimes when I ask for clarity we realize that there's been a disconnect and that he was operating under different assumptions or goals than I was. That doesn't happen very often, but the consequences could be major, including losing the trust of our clients if he adds something to a document that runs counter to how the partnership has been represented.

You need to manage your financial advisor the same way. While financial planners have more expertise in financial planning than you do, it's still *your* money, and no one cares about it or knows what you want to ultimately do with it the way you do. Your advisor is working *for* you, and you need to make sure that you both communicate your needs. You also need to verify that your advisor's recommendations, if you aren't clear on some of them, meet your needs. Here are some guidelines to follow:

**1. Always prioritize building emergency savings, maximizing your employer's tax-advantaged accounts, and paying off high-interest-rate debt over investing with your advisor.** The one exception is rolling over a previous employer's plan to an IRA with an advisor. As we discussed in previous chapters, each of these priorities can provide more "bang for your buck" than even the best advisor's investment strategy.

**2. Make sure your advisor understands you, your goals, and your values.** It's important to establish as much of this understanding as possible up-front, but you'll want to continue the conversation with quarterly or at least annual meetings to make sure everything remains in line with your expectations and to update your advisor on any changes in your goals or situation. Financial planning is a process, not a one-time event.

**3. Don't forget to involve your spouse or partner.** Even if you tend to manage the family finances, it's important for your spouse to build a relationship with your advisor, especially in case something happens to you. It could also be a good idea to involve your children once they're old enough. After all, we don't live forever.

**4. Make sure your advisor is incorporating your employee benefits into your investment plan.** For example, you may not need to purchase insurance that you already have through work. Ideally, your advisor will complement what you have in your employer's retirement account by prioritizing more tax-inefficient investments, such as corporate bonds, REITs (real estate investment trusts), and high-turnover stock funds, in your tax-sheltered accounts.

**5. Introduce your financial planner to your other advisors.**

All of your advisors should have good working relationships and understand what each is doing so they're not missing anything or working at cross-purposes.

## WHEN SHOULD YOU FIRE YOUR ADVISOR?

If you are managing your advisor well, it should be clear whether that person is worth the fees you are paying or whether you are wasting your time and money. Far too many people fire their advisor based on short-term performance, when the advisor might actually be doing exactly the right thing for them, based on their goals. For example, in 1999 most advisors who were working with conservative investors limited their exposure to tech stocks. In fact, I was running a hedge fund at that time, focused on established companies with sound brands and financials and eschewing investments I felt had undue risk for the same reason other advisors avoided dot-com stocks — my investors were already wealthy and wanted to stay that way. They wanted to protect their assets first and foremost.

Looking at the returns achieved by this conservative investment strategy in 1999, you'd see that they were miserable compared with returns from investing in dot-com stocks. But in 2000, after the technology bubble burst and the stock market crashed, conservative investors ended up with minor losses compared with the losses for those who had taken more risk. The absolute wrong thing for a conservative investor to do in 1999 would have been to fire an advisor who was investing his assets conservatively and take his money to an advisor who was getting an exceptional return investing in dot-com stocks — which were just about to plummet.

So, if it's not about short-term performance, how do you evaluate whether your advisor is an asset to your finances or an anchor holding down performance?

Here's a process that we've recommended to thousands of investors struggling with this issue. Over the long term, it has enhanced their returns and reduced their risk by ensuring that they make informed decisions about whether to keep or ditch their advisor:

**1. Your advisor should be focused more on you and your goals than on your portfolio's short-term performance.** That usually begins with having a written investment policy statement based on your time frame and risk tolerance. If your advisor doesn't have an investment policy statement or is chasing the latest fad instead of following your agreed-upon policy, you may need to find a new advisor.

**2. Whenever you have concerns, you should be able to call your advisor and have an open and honest dialogue about those concerns.** Lack of communication is one of the biggest complaints people have about their advisors. If you have this problem, it's a major reason for switching.

**3. Your advisor shouldn't just be an enabler.** One of the most valuable services an advisor can provide is to serve as an objective and knowledgeable check on our worst instincts. In other words, we want our advisors to try to talk us out of doing something stupid or rash with our money. Yes, of course, it's your money and you make the final decision, but your advisor at least owes you an honest opinion based on his or her professional judgment and experience. After all, that's what you're paying for.

This and the previous chapters have focused on what you as an individual can do to make a difference in your personal finances. The next chapter will address what we *all* can do to make a collective difference in the way things are done.

# 9

## Holistic Wealth: The Path to Financial (and Physical) Health

**Let's say you've** found the perfect financial advisor, one who puts your needs ahead of his or her own when investing and protecting your money. Congratulations! You've done something great for yourself and for your future. This is an important milestone, and you have good cause to celebrate.

Just make sure you don't fall into the trap that so many people do of thinking that "now everything is taken care of." You can never lose sight of the fact that no one cares about your money more than you do, not even the best financial advisor. And even with the best financial advisor, there will always be areas of your finances that you'll tend to yourself, because your advisor is compensated only for managing your investments, not your whole financial picture.

You will need to find a way to bridge this gap. This chapter will help you do that by providing you with the resources to make decisions in the important areas of your financial life that an advisor can't help you with. It will also help you achieve the most important goal of all when it comes to your finances: figuring out what financial health means to you and what you are willing to do to achieve it.

Remember those commercials with the eggs? "This is your brain" (shot of an egg). "This is your brain on drugs" (shot of an egg in a frying pan). I know I'm dating myself with this reference (if you never saw the commercial, you can find it on YouTube), but that's where my mind goes every time I think of the average American's real financial situation versus how a financial advisor sees it.

This is your real financial situation:

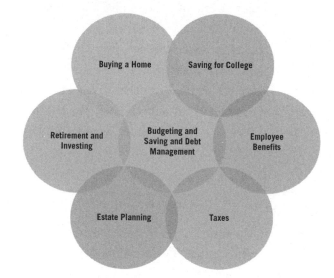

This is how a financial advisor sees your financial situation:

And therein lies the problem—and the reason I decided to write this book.

• • •

When you look at your finances, you see the life you have now and the life you hope to have in the future. But when an advisor looks at your finances, he or she sees your investable assets (money outside of what you are already investing or spending) and how those assets could grow over time.

The problem is that, at the end of the day, investable assets are a very small piece of the financial picture for most Americans. Any outside investments they have are mainly there to supplement their financial security after they have taken full advantage of their employer's benefits.

The other problem is that over half a million financial professionals in this country are incentivized to promote their services as the best way for you to achieve financial security. Forget all of your free, discounted, and tax-favorable employee benefits. Forget paying off that high-interest-rate debt that's costing you over 20 percent per year. Forget that dream home. Forget all the financial transactions you make every day—earning, buying, selling, borrowing, withdrawing—along with those key turning-point decisions: Should I get married? Are we ready to have a baby? Or even, is it time to get a dog? Forget that emergency savings fund, raising financially responsible kids, and finding good but cost-effective health care.

The disconnect doesn't end there. Because advisors are motivated to view and value their clients based on the amount those clients can generate in fees and commissions, they are inclined to view you as nothing more than an investment portfolio. That can compromise their ability to fully relate to you on a personal level. As a result, too many advisors miss one of the most pervasive problems people face.

Daily financial stress.

## FINANCIAL STRESS CAN LITERALLY KILL YOU

If you are like most people, every time you think about your finances you probably feel at least some degree of stress. According to our latest research, a whopping 85 percent of Americans say they suffer from financial stress, and that includes people of all ages and income levels. Even more remarkable is that 73 percent of those who earn $200,000 or more per year claim to be financially stressed, even though many of us look at them and wish we had a paycheck even half as large as theirs!

Financial stress takes a toll on the body. People who are financially stressed are much more likely to suffer from serious, even life-threatening, medical conditions. According to a recent study by the Associated Press and AOL, people with high levels of financial stress are twice as likely to have heart attacks than those under low levels of financial stress. Those under high levels of financial stress are also more than seven times as likely to suffer from severe anxiety, nearly six times as likely to suffer from severe depression, more than twice as likely to suffer from insomnia, and over three times as likely to suffer from stomach ulcers. They also tend to have higher blood pressure, which coupled with many of the above conditions, puts them at much greater risk for serious disease over time. The Personal Finance Employee Education Foundation has found that employees who have significant financial stress have 24 percent higher health care costs than the overall population (which of course further exacerbates their financial stress).

Financial stress is one of the most damaging stressors to your body because it's an ongoing stress (at least until you resolve your financial problems), as opposed to a temporary stress. Whenever you get significantly stressed, your body releases more of a hormone called cortisol—which is meant to be reserved for "fight-or-flight" situations. It provides a quick burst of energy to draw upon reserves of strength and urgency to prevail in life-or-death situations. You've probably heard stories of people who were able to perform amazing feats of strength in an emergency—lifting cars off people or running miles beyond their normal capacity. This happened because their bodies responded to stress hormones and kicked into high gear.

Over short periods of time, cortisol gives us strength. As with a shot of adrenaline, however, we're not meant to be exposed to it over the long term, day in and day out. When your body is flooded with cortisol every single day because you are stressed about money, your body eventually starts to break down. Instead of energizing you, cortisol actually begins to do just the opposite: it wears you out, and your health breaks down.

Scientific studies have validated the correlation between financial stress and physical disease. We see this correlation every day when people who are clearly in a downward cycle of financial stress call our financial helpline. Their stress may have already caused illness, performance problems on the job, and even divorce. These issues in turn cause more financial stress, which exacerbates their medical, job performance, and relationship issues, and the cycle goes on and on. Here's just one story from the many people who have called us because they were stuck in a cycle of serious financial stress that was affecting far more than just their money—it was ruining their lives.

Ana called our financial helpline on the verge of tears. She had just been diagnosed with type 2 diabetes—a result of gaining 45 pounds since her last checkup. Just a few years earlier, she'd been a long-distance runner in great shape, but then her husband lost his job and she had to stop running so she could work overtime to make ends meet. Even with the overtime, her income couldn't even come close to replacing his income, and their financial situation got progressively worse. Eventually her husband ran out of unemployment benefits, and their debts began to skyrocket. She started having migraines and panic attacks, which limited the number of hours she could work at a time when her family needed money more than ever.

When she called us, not only was she fearing that her house was about to be foreclosed on, but she was seriously considering divorce and facing the high cost of medication for her diabetes if she didn't drastically change her diet and lifestyle. The doctor told her that stress was causing her weight gain and also compromising her body's ability to produce insulin, which regulates blood sugar. He gave her referrals to expensive personal trainers and nutritionists, not realizing that it was *financial* stress that was causing all her problems in the first place!

On top of all this, she had three children to care for and desperately wanted them to have a better life than she'd had growing up. With her marriage hanging by a thread, her health compromised, her home on the line, and the overwhelming pressure to keep everything together for her children, she called us as a last resort.

The good news is that ultimately we were able to help Ana. We began by providing an outlet for all her pent-up frustration, and then we *triaged* her financial issues—a term she was familiar with from working in a children's hospital. Just as she had regularly prioritized patients who had the most urgent and serious medical needs over those with less serious problems, we tackled her most pressing financial issues first.

Our financial planner helped her come up with money to save her home by selling possessions she didn't need and then renting her guest bedroom to a fellow nurse. The added income helped Ana pay her mortgage.

From there, he worked with her weekly, isolating and facing each of her financial challenges and helping her figure out what she could do to solve it. It was a yearlong process until Ana was fully back on her feet financially, with her debts under control, her house payments current, and a small emergency fund in place to tide the family over in the event of unexpected expenses. But getting her financial house in order was actually only a small part of Ana's transformation.

As she began to take control of her finances, Ana regained confidence and experienced a sense of relief. She could see the light at the end of the tunnel, and this alone began to reduce her stress considerably. Once her brain went from panic mode to problem-solving mode, she relied less and less on her financial coach to come up with solutions to her problems and began to think of them on her own.

Her positive change in attitude affected her husband, who began to see that he too could take control of his situation. He enrolled in a career counseling program and ultimately found a job helping others in a job placement firm. This new work was meaningful to him, and it paid just as much as his previous job in marketing, which he'd never really liked all that much anyway. His reemployment obviously helped the couple's finances immensely, and it wasn't long before they were totally out of credit card debt. Ana even began volunteering to teach classes on reducing debt at her church so that she could help others going through the same sort of struggles she had just overcome.

As Ana's stress levels progressively improved, she had fewer and fewer migraines and panic attacks, until they disappeared altogether. She also found the extra weight dropping off, even though she never made an appointment with any of the personal trainers or nutritionists her doctor had recommended.

People very commonly lose weight when they reduce their stress, because cortisol tends to slow down your metabolism and increase your hunger. When Ana went to the doctor a year and a half later for her annual checkup, her blood sugar levels were on their way back to normal and she had taken control of her diabetes without having to take expensive prescription drugs.

## How Much Is Your Financial Stress Costing You?

Think about it for a minute. How much is your financial stress costing you? How much healthier would you be if you didn't have to worry about money again because you were financially secure? How much better would you sleep at night? How much healthier would you be? How much better would your relationships be? How much better would you perform at work without having the distraction of worrying about money?

Once the burden of financial worries is lifted, we often find that we have the mental freedom to figure out our next career path. For many of us, that's a luxury we never had until we eliminated daily financial stress from our lives.

## NEW AND BETTER MODELS TO MEET YOUR NEEDS

The good news is that new services are emerging to provide holistic financial guidance to all Americans, regardless of their financial situation.

They're part of a new developing industry known as "financial wellness," and it's growing rapidly. In this field, financial planners work with you, with no conflicts of interest, as financial coaches who can help you improve your financial health in all areas of your life.

Imagine how different your life would be if the following services were available to you:

- Your advisor works with you to help you find ways to save that extra $1, $3, $5, or $10 a day that will ultimately help you build the life you want.
- Your advisor helps you negotiate with your creditors to reduce your debt and improve your credit rating so that you are eligible for better interest rates on mortgages, student loans, or small business loans.
- Your advisor helps you find scholarships to send your children to college without having to pay tuition out of pocket or take out a loan—or at the very least, reducing the amount you need to pay or borrow.
- Your advisor works with you to navigate through all your different company benefits and helps you make the best decisions about how to leverage these benefits to achieve your most important financial goals.
- Your advisor helps you with health care planning, making sure that you choose the right health insurance and fund your HSA adequately.
- Your advisor reviews financial recommendations you get from other advisors who are vying for your business and helps you evaluate them so that you make the decisions that enhance your financial security.
- Your advisor looks at your finances and helps you understand when it's the right time to buy a home and how much you really can afford to pay. (How useful would that have been in 2007, when so many people purchased homes they couldn't afford once the interest rate reset?)

- Your advisor helps you find affordable long-term care options for your parents, even if they don't have medical insurance.
- Your advisor works with you and your spouse to develop a financially lucrative partnership and even helps you teach your kids how to become financially responsible.

How different would your life be if your advisor did all this? How much less stress would you have? How much more financially secure would you be?

These are the services offered by financial wellness advisors. And the best news yet is that some employees can access these services free of charge through their employer—yet another one of the benefits your "best financial services provider" might offer.

## RESOURCES TO HELP YOU IMPROVE YOUR FINANCIAL HEALTH

**1. Workplace financial wellness programs.** Recognizing the connection between financial stress and physical illness, more and more employers are expanding their physical wellness programs to include financial wellness as an additional employee benefit. The best workplace financial wellness programs are designed to address all your financial needs through an ongoing program that provides you with the personalized support you need to progressively improve your financial health. Programs typically combine a personalized financial wellness assessment (a financial scale of sorts to gauge your overall financial health so that you know where you stand) with unlimited access to a financial planner who works with you as your personal financial coach.

This industry is still relatively new, so you have to be careful and make sure that what your employer is promoting as financial wellness really is designed to help employees become more financially healthy, not to line the pockets of an advisor who uses "financial wellness" as a guise for selling financial products and services. A true financial wellness program should be delivered by a company that doesn't sell any financial products or services and doesn't manage any money. The company's sole source of revenue should be from the sale of financial education (and potentially other types of wellness programs) to companies, which pay for the service as a benefit to employees.

The program should also fully integrate all of your financial benefits, so that you have all the total support you need to maximize these benefits.

**2. Financial wellness packages (sold directly to individuals).** A growing number of companies focus on providing unbiased financial guidance to individuals, typically for a relatively low monthly subscription fee. These services offer a financial wellness package that includes unlimited access to online tools and sophisticated mobile apps that can help you organize your finances and manage your spending, coupled with scheduled phone calls with a financial coach. As with corporate financial wellness programs, it's critical to make sure that the company you're considering has no conflicts of interest. Any company that promotes a "financial wellness package" should be independently owned and operated, not affiliated with a broker-dealer or any financial services firm. You should pay a flat monthly or annual fee for access to a planner who works full-time as a financial educator or coach.

To find companies that sell individual financial wellness packages, simply google "financial wellness programs."

**3. Fee-only financial planners.** When I speak of financial advisors in this book, I'm talking about the vast majority of financial advisors who are compensated by selling you financial products or services or managing your money. They represent most of the financial advisors active in the United States today. A lesser-known alternative is a "fee-only" financial advisor who charges an hourly rate or retainer, and who really does address your financial situation holistically. That's because these advisors are compensated solely for their time, not through a commission on the financial products or services they sell or a percentage of the amount of money they manage.

If no financial wellness program available through your employer is sufficient for your needs, and if you feel that you wouldn't get enough support from simply purchasing a financial wellness package from a financial wellness firm, a fee-only advisor who charges an hourly rate or annual retainer could be a great alternative for you.

The biggest downside is that these professionals are expensive — typically they charge $150 or more per hour — so you really have to make good use of your time with them. Also, because of the cost, they are sometimes a better fit financially for high-income and high-net-worth individuals who want an unbiased perspective on managing, investing, and protecting their assets. An advisor who operates under this compensation structure might cost people in this situation significantly less than what they would otherwise pay in commissions or fees to a more traditional financial planner.

To find a fee-only planner who charges an hourly rate or an annual retainer, go to the website of the Garrett Planning Network (garrettplanningnetwork.com), or the Alliance of Comprehensive Planners (acplanners.org).

Please keep in mind that not having the same conflicts of interest faced by traditional planners does not necessarily make a fee-only advisor who charges a flat rate or hourly fee an excellent financial planner. You will still want to put the advisors you consider through a rigorous selection process, asking them about their background, credentials, client references (including clients who no longer use their services), and fees and requesting a full listing of the services they provide.

**4. Nonprofit organizations that provide financial education, typically through workshops and financial counseling.** An increasing number of people who have left the financial services industry are turning to financial education in the hope of coming up with a better solution for people who need financial help but can't afford it. As a result, the number of nonprofit organizations that offer financial education is growing. Some of the better ones are the National Endowment for Financial Education (NEFE); Jump$tart, an organization that focuses on bringing financial education to schools but also sponsors adult financial education initiatives; and the Women's Institute for a Secure Retirement (WISER), an organization that helps women become more financially secure. All of these organizations provide unbiased financial education materials.

Your local community may also make financial workshops available for free. Just make sure that the instructor has no conflicts of interest and is there to educate you rather than to promote specific products or services.

## MAKE THE MIND SHIFT: BECOME FINANCIALLY FIT FOR LIFE

It's important to remember that even though a financial wellness program can provide you with guidance and support you can't get from a financial planner, you still have to do the work to create a financially healthy lifestyle for yourself and your family. Your financial coach can guide you, but it's up to you to take his or her guidance and integrate it into your life.

Let's go back to Ana's story. Our financial planner got her going in the right direction and helped her change her perspective about her finances. But Ana was the one who did the hard work. She was the one who rented out her guest bedroom to one of her coworkers, who inspired her husband by setting a good example, who progressively paid down her debts until she and her husband were debt-free, who established an emergency fund, and who then chose to pay it all forward by teaching classes at her church to help others who were struggling financially. Ana is the hero of her story, and you are the hero of your story as well. There are resources you can turn to for help, but only you can do it for yourself.

## FINDING THE RIGHT BALANCE

If you do want to change anything about your financial situation, you have one question to answer right now: how badly do you want it?

Let me explain with this personal story. Three years ago, I reached a point where I was about 30 pounds overweight. For most of my life I'd been one of those annoying people who didn't worry about her weight. I was an athlete through school, and I carried that mind-set through into adulthood: I ate what I wanted, when I wanted, without any regard for calories, fat, or carbs. I didn't view food as having an impact on my weight, my health, or my overall well-being.

Then I went through a series of setbacks, one on top of the other. A good friend stole from me and my mom was diagnosed with a terminal illness. I thought I was handling it all, but I wasn't. I stopped exercising and, without realizing it, turned to food for comfort. After all, I was one of those lucky people who could eat whatever she wanted! Or so I thought.

Thirty-plus pounds later, I woke up one day and realized I was seriously "bloated." No kidding. That was my conclusion (which my husband, bless his heart, supported out of a sense of self-preservation). When I had to get my wedding ring *cut off my finger,* I thought the problem was an allergic reaction!

Finally, after none of my clothes fit anymore, I stepped on a scale and was shocked at what it said. Certain it was not calibrated correctly, and still in denial, I stepped on two more scales—only to find out that the first scale was actually the most forgiving!

I turned to a good friend who had struggled with her weight until she reached adulthood and subsequently changed her entire lifestyle. I cried, I whined. I was sure it was early menopause. It wasn't fair—I was not a chronic "overeater." Why was this happening to me? Why now when my heart was breaking?

She let me whine over most of our lunch. And then she said something I will never forget.

"Do you realize you just ate 1,500 calories? That's more than I can eat in a day if I want to maintain my weight."

I looked at the empty dish of calamari and my half-eaten hamburger and cheese fries dripping with ranch dressing and then looked at her salad, still on her plate, and realized, with a combination of shame and anger, that I wasn't a victim after all. I had been eating with abandon, and I was picking foods that were both really fattening and really bad for me.

After asking my friend to be my "nutritionist," I proceeded to challenge everything she said about what I should eat, even after she pulled out her copy of Jillian Michaels's book *Master Your Metabolism,* which went into painful detail about what it takes to be truly physically fit.

I thought there just *had* to be an easier, faster way to shed the pounds. I became a vegan for six hours—before I took an ice cream break and gave up on that diet from then on. Then I became a "modified vegan," which really meant eating some vegan foods plus whatever else I wanted. When that didn't work, I tried (don't laugh) a "cookie diet." I thought they were cookies, but they were actually diet protein bars shaped like cookies. I was starving the entire time. That lasted three days before I realized I had a decision to make.

I needed to get real and be honest with myself about why I wanted to lose the weight. How much was I *really* willing to sacrifice, and what was truly realistic for me to expect based on the work I was willing to put in? Where was that balance where the changes I was willing to make were worth all the sacrifice in the end?

I looked at my son and husband and decided that what I really wanted was simply to be healthier, which included losing weight, but also eating healthier, exercising like the athlete I had been most of my life, and finding ways to manage my stress. I returned to my "nutritionist" friend, apologized, and let her know what I wanted and what I was willing to do to get it. Once I clarified that I wasn't striving to be 108 pounds, her diet suggestions suddenly became much more appealing!

No more cookie diets. No more short-term veganism. I simply started eating better—fewer simple carbs, more vegetables, more meals with smaller portions, and a one-hour walk every day (which also helped my stress). The weight was painfully slow to come off at first, but as I got more used to my new lifestyle, I was able to make more positive changes and it started to come off faster.

Eventually, I stopped looking at the scale as the ultimate measurement and instead focused more on my overall health and well-being. I knew I was continuing to lose weight because I was fitting into my "skinny" clothes again, but that became an almost ancillary benefit, a by-product of something much bigger—living a healthy lifestyle was making me a better, happier, more loving, and more fulfilled person.

*This same concept applies to your financial health.* Of course, it would be lovely to be wealthy beyond imagination, but is it really worth putting in too many hours a week at a job you don't love, depriving yourself of all the things that give you joy and comfort, and obsessing daily over how your investments are performing? For most people, the answer is no.

Financial experts like to tell you that you should spend less, save more, and cut out all unnecessary expenses. The more you deprive yourself today, they say, the better your future will be. When you do the math, you see that they're technically correct, but the reality is that following a plan that you detest—that causes you to feel deprived every single day—is almost never sustainable. Going back to the concept of extreme retirement—saving half or more of your money to become financially secure and independent by your thirties or forties—we're reminded that extreme plans work only for people who can be happy and fulfilled living very frugal lives (and who may even secretly enjoy it). Many more of us would give up on an extreme plan, feeling like a failure and spending more than we did before we started, to make up for the deprivation we've put ourselves through.

Even if you can sustain an extreme financial plan and become wealthy, what you've really become, in my book, is the financial equivalent of an anorexic—wealthy maybe, but not financially healthy. Financial health brings a sense of peace and fulfillment, and anyone who lives a life of deprivation will never achieve these things.

So before you work with a financial coach, enroll in a financial wellness program, or hire a financial advisor, make sure you know what you really want out of the whole process.

- **Where are you now financially?** What is the unvarnished reality of your situation? (Answering this question is akin to stepping on the scale.)
- **Where do you want to be financially to ultimately have a life free of financial stress?** Focus on what will give you peace of mind and the freedom to live life on your own terms, rather than a dollar figure you've decided will mean you've "succeeded in life." (In other words, give up the concept of reaching "108 pounds" and instead focus on becoming healthy.)
- **What are your limitations and boundaries?** How far are you willing to go to achieve the life you want, and how far is too far? Know what you are *not* willing to do or tolerate. Where do you draw the line? What is simply too much of a sacrifice, too much risk to be worth it, or too much money to pay for the chance of a better return? Sometimes drawing the line does more than set us up for success—it protects us from others who might otherwise lead us astray.

Contrary to what society likes to tell us, wealth is not a number. It's the ability to live the life you want and to find meaning and wisdom in the journey you take to get there.

# 10

## Follow the Money Trail to a Better Financial Future

**Nina couldn't believe** she had joined the PTA. Didn't she used to make fun of those kinds of moms back in college? Her son had just entered kindergarten, and it was both surreal and quite exciting that she was now going to her first PTA meeting, not knowing what to expect or what she was supposed to do.

Nina sat in the circle as the PTA president introduced the guest speaker, a gentleman named Adam, who was flanked by his two associates. The first meeting of the school year seemed like a perfect time to discuss college savings, explained the PTA president. Then, without further ado, she gave the floor to Adam. He told the tale of how he, now in his late fifties, had been planning the college educations of his three children since they were born. And good thing, because by the time his third would be going off to college in a few years, he was going to have spent at least a quarter of a million dollars.

"How many people here have already set up a 529?" he asked, looking for a show of hands. Nina was relieved when she saw only two women raise theirs. Nina and her husband had debated this possibility long ago, but decided that they could hardly contribute to their own retirement, never mind a 529 for college savings. Not yet at least.

Adam wasn't surprised that only a small minority were already preparing for college. Then he asked: did they know that by the time their little five-year-olds were college age, parents would be expected to shell out $1 million for college?

"What?!" Nina gasped in the direction of the woman next to her. This was stunning news. Nina challenged Adam, explaining that she and her husband were prioritizing saving in their respective 401(k) plans, since they were getting free money from their employers in matching contributions. She also said that if worse came to worst, she knew her children could get financial aid and perhaps scholarships as well, but that there was no such thing for retirement savings.

Adam's response sent a chill down her spine. "So you are putting yourself ahead of your children? Well, I guess if those are your values . . ." He let the thought linger, and Nina watched as looks of disgust crossed the faces of the other parents. She had officially—and inadvertently—become the pariah of the entire school—or at least of classroom 108. Visions of canceled playdates flooded her mind, and she even felt disgusted with herself.

As the murmurs of the group turned into loud chatter, Adam told the parents that he knew how important their children were to them—implying, once again, that Nina was an irresponsible parent for investing in her 401(k) instead of a 529 plan for her children's college educations. He added that he could absolutely help them secure a bright future for their children and urged them to take his card and call him anytime with questions. On the business card, beneath the well-known masthead of a national wealth management company, was Adam's title: Financial Advisor.

Fortunately, Nina followed the money trail and asked the PTA president how this guest came to be invited to speak. The president said, "We got an email from him asking to speak with the group on this important topic of financial planning, so we thought we were providing a benefit."

Unfortunately for the PTA, the only benefit to be had was going to be on behalf of Adam.

## FAST-FOOD FINANCE: WOULD YOU LIKE LIES WITH THAT?

Adam is an example of what is wrong with the financial system. Fortunately, advisors who are true financial planners, rather than brokers trying to make a quick sale, would never use the kind of scare tactic Adam used at the PTA meeting. But the reality is that Adam had three kids of his own to put through school and a wife who wanted a nice lifestyle. The easiest way for him to find new clients was to give talks at local schools and worry naive parents into taking all the money they could find (including taking out second mortgages on their homes, drawing cash advances from their credit cards, and raiding their retirement plans) in order to invest their money in the expensive mutual funds he sold as part of his "college savings" spiel. In other words, his top priority was himself and his family, not his clients.

We like to think that there's a sense of karma in the world—that if you work hard and do right by others, you will be rewarded in turn. Unfortunately, the financial services industry didn't get this memo. The fastest way for financial advisors to make money is often at the expense of the clients they're supposed to serve. Indeed, far too often they're playing a zero-sum game—your financial security or their own—and because they also have families to feed and mortgages to pay, theirs wins.

This chapter's purpose is to help you understand how the financial services system is set up to operate, why it is a failing system for most people, and how you can become part of the growing movement to fix it. You'll learn how to avoid (and how to help others avoid) the pervasive "Fast-Food Finance" mentality: a seemingly polished person like Adam appears to be trying to help you set up a 529 plan but upsells you with products and services on the side instead—sort of like fries and a Coke, except in this case the "fast food" is loaded with high sales commissions hidden in the fine print.

In the financial industry, this is called "information selling": these salespeople seem to be focusing on something you care about deeply—

in this case, the future of your children—but are simply using your emotional need as a lure to find ancillary ways to gather more of your money. You obviously don't want or need that kind of approach. In the last chapter, I defined true financial wellness and the plethora of benefits of achieving and sustaining wellness far beyond the wallet. Taking the one-and-done approach of Fast-Food Finance—signing on the dotted line and giving the advisor approval to set up the lead product, "and then some"—is the antithesis of financial wellness. True financial wellness recognizes that you are more than a 401(k) plan statement, a 529 college savings plan, or a life insurance policy.

Still, the system is so confusing and clarity so elusive that even the savviest people, like Nina, find it difficult to navigate it or decipher what they want to accomplish, what they need to accomplish, and the difference between the two (and there might very well be a significant difference). Why does the financial services industry seem to be stacked against the average person? And more importantly, why is it allowed to operate this way?

For answers, follow the money trail.

## THE BUSINESS OF BIAS

There are several models in the financial services industry, but the thread that connects them all is bias—a focus on leading consumers to products and services that are sellable for money. As long as there is money at the end of the trail, the advisor has an interest in leading you down it. It's business, after all. No Volvo dealer is going to tell you to buy a Mazda when he only stands to make a commission at the Volvo dealership. If you look at any industry, you'll see the golden handcuffs on almost everyone at one point or another.

But the difference is that the Volvo dealer is not holding himself or herself out to be a "car-buying consultant" who can help you find the best type of car for your situation. Consumers know what they are getting into when they go to a dealership to purchase a car, and most have already done their homework ahead of time. In short, they know that the Volvo dealer sells only Volvos, not competing cars. It's the rare car dealer who would look at your individual needs and suggest that you would be better off purchasing another brand of car rather than one of his cars.

Unfortunately, the average consumer who invests money with a financial advisor is often not aware that the advisor is really a financial salesperson commissioned to sell specific investments from a particular financial services company. In short, he *may not be a true financial planner* focused on helping clients make the best possible financial decisions based on their personal situation.

And this is a huge problem when you consider what's at stake. You are responsible for your money, and there can be severe consequences when you punt on that responsibility. This is why it's important to be aware of your various financial options, how they fit your situation, and which one you should consider, all based on your own needs. Understanding your options will help you better understand the motivations behind certain recommendations and will raise red flags for you when a recommendation doesn't seem to line up with your goals so much as to line the advisor's wallet.

Most financial institutions operate according to one of the following revenue models: commissions, fee-only retainer, fee-based assets under management, hourly fees only, fee-only assets under management, fee for service, or a combination of these models. In this chapter, we'll cover the three most prevalent models: commission-based, fee-based assets under management, and hourly.

## The Commission-Based Model

In a commission-based model, advisors get paid only when they sell certain investments or insurance policies. This approach is the one most prone to posing a conflict of interest. A commission-based advisor might tell you something like, "You only pay this once and then you never have to pay it again." While that may be true, you will have to pay that fee on each successive investment, and these investments may have above-average ongoing costs as well.

Or you may find yourself getting calls, particularly at the end of the month, "encouraging" you to add money to your existing investments or even to consider a new investment. Here's what's going on: commission-based advisors must meet their monthly quota in order to stay on with their company. If they miss their monthly quota, then insurance premiums aren't covered and bonuses aren't paid out. This definitely incentivizes them to sell something, anything, before the end of the month.

A commission-based model also influences how advisors are trained. These advisors are taught to create a sense of urgency, and not just in you—you may be receiving that call at the end of the month because he needs a commission *now*. Or you may be deterred by your advisor from making a transaction because he feels it's not a good move. But is he steering you away from this choice because there is simply no commission to be made off it? Or because he doesn't have access to that choice? Perhaps he won't make his sales quota that month if he offers that choice. Or maybe this advisor simply doesn't know about the choice you are inquiring about. As you can see, this is tricky territory.

Commission-based models are typically the most expensive, the most riddled with conflicts of interest, and the ones that can steer you in the wrong direction financially. That said, if you have done your homework and are simply using a commission-based financial advisor to purchase a financial product or service that you know you need, this is no different than going into a Volvo dealer, having researched all your options, to purchase a specific Volvo make and model you've decided upon ahead of time. In this case, the commission-based advisor is not steering you in a specific direction—you are the one doing the steering.

## The Assets Under Management Model

In an assets under management model, the advisor gets paid for managing assets for a fee, typically an average of 1 percent of the money you invest on an annual basis, though the rate can vary considerably based on how much you invest. This is a cleaner model than commission-based because the advisor can choose from the whole universe of mutual funds to create a portfolio that is best suited to your needs; an assets under management advisor isn't "chained" to recommending the specific mutual funds offered by his or her firm. In theory, the advisor is incentivized to make your portfolio grow because, as your account gets larger, the advisor gets a percentage of a larger balance. Even here, however, there are some major conflicts of interest to be aware of.

First, advisors under this model have every incentive to manage as much of your money as possible. The more ruthless among them may suggest that you take the money you have invested in your employee benefits, like your retirement plan, and invest with them instead. Or worse, they might encourage you to effectively go into debt by borrowing against your home or tapping other sources of credit to come up with more money that you can turn over to them to invest on your behalf.

This is a significant problem, in particular for retirees, who may be best served by leaving their money in their retirement plan until they are ready to withdraw those assets. Instead, they are encouraged to "roll over" those assets to an advisor who will charge them higher fees than they were paying for their investments in their company's plan (which typically will have more reasonable fees).

There are four other issues with the assets under management model:

**1. This model overwhelmingly favors the wealthy because the more their clients invest, the more money advisors make.** As a result, many advisors have "minimum" requirements and will not help those who have less than a certain amount of assets. That minimum is often $100,000, but sometimes it's as high as $1 million or more.

**2. If the amount you invest is at the minimum requirement, or close to it, you will probably be charged a higher percentage of assets, and that charge can drag down your return.** You also may not get the personalized attention you need—the reality is that the advisor has only so much time and would rather focus on larger accounts.

**3. You pay the advisory fee even when your account trails the market or loses money.** That's right, that fee is deducted from your account even if your advisor chose funds that underperform or lose money. In other words, *regardless of whether your advisor makes or loses money for you, he gets paid.*

**4. Most assets under management advisors also charge commissions on insurance, annuities, and other financial products or services designed to protect your wealth or convert a lump sum into a monthly stream of income.** Many people who invest with an advisor who uses this model may not realize they are also paying commissions for other services. Be sure to ask your advisor up-front about these other fees.

### The Hourly Fee-Only Model

Fee-only is my favorite model of the lot. In this model, advisors charge for their financial planning services but earn no fees or commissions based on the amount you invest or the specific investments you choose. In short, you pay them a straight fee for their services based on the amount of time they spend helping you. And because these advisors are charging to help you create and implement a strong financial plan, their interests are aligned with yours. This model also tends to be the most holistic, as your advisor is free to spend more time on your entire financial life, not just the products and services he or she needs to sell to collect a commission. Advisors who take this kind of approach spend time looking for a solution that's right for you. The result can be a more customized approach to achieving true financial wellness.

Here's the bad news, though: the fee-only model, the one that is in the customer's best interest, in reality is struggling to survive. I do not personally know one fee-only planner who has been able to stay in business longer than seven years without reverting to a different model or joining a financial services firm where they are paid in more traditional ways. Why?

Maybe people are uncomfortable writing out a check up-front, or even after services are rendered. Psychologically, of course, it's hard to part with a large sum of money. Yet most investors are already paying out thousands of dollars or more in commissions to receive biased advice that is not helping their situation in the long run. Presumably, they are somehow more comfortable with fees being taken quietly from their account by their advisor. I know, it doesn't make much sense, but that seems to be what's going on. In short, how much of our money are we paying out in order *not* to write a check?

## WHAT YOUR FINANCIAL ADVISOR ISN'T TELLING YOU

Advisors who tell you they are offering you a financial plan for "free" are probably not telling you that they are trained to use a "financial plan" as a way to learn more about your assets so they can share that information with their firm. Trained to believe that their own firm is superior to all others, they justify this sales protocol as necessary in order to save their clients from "horrible" other companies. Some advisors are all about rescuing you from competitors that will harm you, but then they're free to move to those competitors when the compensation looks better there.

What many advisors also don't tell you is that they receive extensive ongoing training from their firm and a stream of firm-recommended "products of the month" to sell to clients. They are trained to make recommendations shaped around these core products, the source of the firm's revenue stream. Every day advisors receive multiple emails from the firm about its financial products and why they should sell these products to their clients. Some emails even give advisors an incentive to sell these products and services to clients by mentioning the commissions or other revenue that will result.

Hundreds of financial advisors employed by major financial services firms have told me that they were explicitly told that their job was not to educate but to advise. For many of these advisors, however, "advising" became synonymous with selling a product or service. The concept of providing unbiased guidance to help someone achieve financial security was pretty much a foreign concept at these firms.

In my opinion, advisor training at the large financial services firms looks something like this: 80 percent is focused on how to sell, especially how to close the sale; 10 percent is training in the products and services available; and another 10 percent is devoted to assessing clients' needs and desires. In other words, advisors at these firms receive zero training in how to provide unbiased financial guidance.

Similarly, I hear regularly from advisors who have been forced to stick to their firm's guidance on a mutual fund recommendation for their clients, even if there are clearly better options. Many of these advisors come to Financial Finesse seeking a job as a financial educator simply because they are frustrated over not being able to focus on what's best for their clients. Instead, they are pressured to put all their efforts into "bringing in clients and assets," because that's how the firm and all its advisors make money.

Many of these advisors *want* to do the right thing, but they are often dissuaded from doing so by the way the industry pays them. They enter the business with the best of intentions, thinking that they can help people create solid financial plans based on their needs and goals. But too many of them end up as financial services salespeople who have to "meet their numbers."

This is simply not right. And it needs to change.

## A BETTER WAY FOR AMERICANS TO GET THE FINANCIAL ADVICE THEY NEED

Even with all the problems that riddle the financial services industry and threaten Americans' long-term financial security, the truth is that we are in a much better place today than when I founded Financial

Finesse in 1999. The movement toward unbiased financial education and advice is accelerating: legislation that protects individual investors is on the rise, business models that align the interests of planners with the interests of their clients have been developed, and a groundswell of people are demanding change.

You can become a part of this "green" (as in "cash") movement to create opportunities for all Americans to have access to the unbiased advice they need to make the right financial decisions for themselves and their families. The following guide describes the actions you can take to join the movement and create the change we so desperately need.

**1. Support new legislation protecting individual investors.** As I write this, President Barack Obama and the US Department of Labor are advocating for legislation that will require all financial advisors to be legally accountable for acting in the best interest of their clients, called the "fiduciary standard." Such a law would ensure that your advisor prioritizes *your* needs over his or her own and takes every step necessary to manage *your* money responsibly. Your advisor would have to recommend the investments that are legitimately best for you, as opposed to limiting recommendations to those investments that generate higher fees and commissions. If your advisor fails to do this, you could take him or her to court.

Implementing this new law would cause a huge shift across the financial services industry and have a major impact. Understandably, the industry has a strong lobby in Congress that has succeeded in squelching similar legislation in the past. I believe that the only way to pass this new legislation is for Americans to come together en masse and demand that Congress put the needs of investors before the needs of the financial services industry.

Another proposal has come from Senator Marco Rubio to open up the federal government's Thrift Savings Plan (TSP) to all American workers who don't have a similar employer-sponsored plan. The TSP is a 401(k)-style savings plan available for federal employees and military personnel that has been widely hailed by retirement experts for its simplicity, diverse investment options, and low costs. This could provide a new tax-advantaged, low-cost option to many people who might otherwise turn to high-fee products or not save for retirement at all.

**2. Advocate for unbiased financial wellness programs as an employee benefit.** At Financial Finesse, we started out helping individuals, only to find that we couldn't stay in business that way. By pure accident, however, we stumbled upon what I believe is the best model to date for Americans, from all walks of life, to get unlimited access to the unbiased financial education and guidance they need, and that is through the workplace, as an employee benefit.

More and more employers are hiring financial education companies, which employ financial planners as full-time educators. These professionals provide personalized guidance, on any and all financial issues, without any of the inherent conflicts of interest of the traditional financial services model. And because the employer pays for the service and the benefit is available to *all* employees, no one is left out. From the CEO to the janitor, every company employee has access to the same benefit, and the financial education company delivering the service gets paid the same, regardless of the individual's financial situation. This arrangement has been the great equalizer in an industry that far too often focuses only on making the wealthy wealthier.

Chances are that your employer already has some sort of financial education in place as a benefit. Ask your HR department what services are available to employees and whether the firm that delivers these services focuses solely on financial education or has a hidden agenda of selling financial products and services to employees. Advocate inside your company for more and better unbiased education if you feel that the available services are not sufficient to help you and your coworkers make the best possible financial decisions with both your benefits and your personal finances.

**3. Get personally involved in your school and community to help people obtain the financial education they need.** You don't have to be a Harvard law professor or a US senator to make a big difference. Candy Lightner was a real estate agent and divorced single mom when her 13-year-old daughter was struck and killed by a drunk driver. Four days after her daughter's death, Lightner started a grassroots organization called Mothers Against Drunk Driving (MADD) to advocate for stiffer penalties for drunk driving. Despite never being involved with reform or politics before, Lightner helped to transform American attitudes toward drunk driving and successfully lead the fight to enact stricter laws across the country. I firmly believe that some of our greatest financial progress will come from passionate individuals who build widespread support through social media and other efforts.

## START WITH SCHOOL

Think of how much further along you would be financially in your life if you had learned what you have learned in this book back in high school. To that end, talk to your local legislature and school board about having mandatory unbiased financial education classes taught in school—by bona fide teachers, not by a financial institution—to help students start their adult lives off on the right track. Such an education program should be highly engaging and should show students the financial impact of their financial decisions and how to build the skills to become financially successful adults.

Special financial education classes should be mandatory for students taking on student loans. It is nothing short of amazing to me that laws exist to ensure that home buyers know exactly what they are paying for a 15- or 30-year mortgage, yet students are mortgaging their futures with no idea of the implications of a $50,000-a-year loan for four years at 5 percent. For the 10-year payoff period, that's about $2,121 per month, which on an average starting salary of about $50,000 (after-tax monthly income of $3,300) means that *over half* of that new college graduate's take-home income will go toward student loan debt. Seeing these numbers in writing might make some students think twice.

## MAKE A DIFFERENCE IN YOUR COMMUNITY

Share what you have learned with your community. Start talking to your friends and family; so many people are in the dark as to what their advisors aren't telling them that you can help fill in many gaps in their knowledge. Start talking with your colleagues at work too. I spoke with one woman who started a financial literacy club at her workplace, almost like a Weight Watchers for debt. Once a week they met over (homemade) lunch to share tips, advice, and encouragement for managing money and getting out of debt. They had an anonymous spreadsheet that tracked everyone's debt and progress toward paying it down, and they reviewed it weekly. After about six months, everyone in the club had paid off at least one debt.

Consider starting a book club focused on money management. (This book would be a great starter book!) Your group could discuss the book chapter by chapter or by topic. With each person in the club offering personal insights, your entire group could collectively help each other make better and more informed money decisions. The club would also encourage all of you to create and stick to better money management habits. Members of the group with better financial habits could mentor others who are struggling.

## A FINAL NOTE

I wrote most of the chapters of this book focusing on you, the individual investor, so that I could inform you personally on how to improve your finances by concentrating on key topics that your advisor isn't telling you about but that you absolutely need to know to be financially successful. The reality, however, is that we are all interconnected, and I urge you to do more than just protect your own financial security. Imagine the impact if every single person who personally improved his or her finances effectively paid it forward, so that all our individual successes could translate into something far bigger than ourselves. Imagine a world where our children and grandchildren had access to all the tools, resources, and advice they needed to become financially secure, even in the worst of economies.

Collectively, we have the power to create this future. Now is the time!

# Appendix:
# Financial Independence Day Checklist

**While it's pretty** much guaranteed that you'll need more than one day to become financially independent, you really don't need much more than that amount of time to set the wheels in motion to change your financial life forever. That's what Financial Independence Day (FID) is meant to mark—a singular allocated day on which you set aside the entire morning and afternoon and commit to thinking about one of the most important, yet usually neglected, aspects of your life—your financial wellness.

When you set aside this one vitally important day, put your "out of the office" alert on your email so that you can totally focus and come face to face with everything from your expenses, debts, income, and investments to your ultimate goals and lifestyle needs. Trust me—taking this day to attend to your financial health is just as critical as taking a sick day when you have the flu. Without it, your financial problems won't resolve on their own, nor will you have a coherent plan for nursing yourself back to financial health.

I encourage you to spend a Financial Independence Day as you would any other day of the year you devote to a vitally important task, whether it be spring-cleaning, back-to-school shopping, or winterizing your car. Pick a date (hopefully soon!) and name it your first annual FID. It's a time for reflection, inspection, and reinvention of all aspects of your financial life.

I hope that won't seem like such a daunting task now that you've read this book. But if setting aside a full workday to focus on your finances just doesn't seem realistic, feel free to break it down into more manageable steps. Dedicate a couple of hours each week, or even each month, to getting your financial house in order. The important thing is that you maintain progress toward achieving your FID.

Either way, you might need a kind of GPS to help you get started, which is what you'll find in the Financial Independence Day Checklist. Personally, I love checklists—for me, there's no better way to prioritize my tasks and boost my confidence. I feel good when I accomplish a task and can cross it off my list. I hope you get just as much satisfaction as I do from using the following checklist to get your FID off to an auspicious start. Pull together all your financial account log-ins, grab your spouse, and get ready to break new financial ground.

*Please note:* This checklist is only a tool. It's how you *use* it to further your financial independence that really matters.

Listed at the end of some of the checklist items are websites that can give you more help and information. The goal is not necessarily to complete every task on the list, but to zero in on those areas where taking important actions will have the biggest impact on your financial situation. This is the way to set yourself up for financial success.

1. **Take control of your spending.**
   - ❑ Determine all the unnecessary expenses you can cut. Be creative. For instance, can you eliminate the gym membership and use workouts from YouTube? Can you cut your satellite service? Look for opportunities to reduce other expenses.
     billcutterz.com
   - ❑ Once you have determined how much you can cut each month, call your payroll department and arrange for that amount to be directly transferred into a savings account. Split those savings between high-interest credit card payments (if needed) and an emergency fund.

❑ Sign up with mint.com or use another system to track your spending and help you stick to your plan.

    mint.com

    yodleemoneycenter.com

## 2. Pay yourself first.

❑ Make sure you're contributing at least enough to your 401(k) or 403(b) retirement plan to maximize the match from your employer.

❑ Sign up for any tax-free accounts offered by your employer, such as a health savings account (HSA) for health care expenses or a flexible spending account (FSA) for dependent care expenses.

## 3. Clean up and protect your credit.

❑ Order your free credit reports so that you can dispute any negative information you may find.

    annualcreditreport.com

❑ Sign up for free credit monitoring and advice.

    creditkarma.com

    creditsesame.com

## 4. Put yourself on the path to being debt-free.

❑ Ask your creditors if they would be willing to lower your interest rate(s). You'll be surprised by how many are willing to do this.

❑ Starting with the highest-interest-rate balances, see if you can refinance your debt with a balance transfer or lower-interest loan.

    creditcards.com

    prosper.com

    lendingclub.com

❑ If you still can't make the minimum payments on your debts, try to negotiate an affordable payment plan with your creditors or schedule an appointment with a nonprofit credit counselor.

    debtadvice.org

    aiccca.com

❏ If you can pay more than the minimum, put your extra payments on the highest-interest or smallest-balance debt and repeat until you've paid off all debt with interest rates above 4 to 6 percent. You can use the DebtBlaster Calculator reproduced on page 33; it's also available online.

ffcalcs.com/debt_blaster

**5. Set up a weekly or monthly appointment with yourself and/or significant other.**

❏ Agree on a date and time in a low-stress environment when you and your partner will check in regularly and review your finances and spending. You could schedule this meeting for a monthly Sunday brunch at home or a biweekly Saturday stroll. You could even communicate electronically via homemade spending logs or Excel spreadsheets.

❏ Review and add to your financial goals, both long-term and short-term, both individual and joint, and set milestones to achieve them within realistic time frames. Check in on your progress during your regular meeting.

**6. Consider working with a financial planner.**

❏ If you don't have an advisor you're happy with and would like help managing your investments, filing your taxes, and/or choosing the right insurance policies, begin by finding out if your employer provides an unbiased financial wellness program that could give you unlimited access to a qualified financial planner to act as your financial coach. If this service isn't available or is insufficient for your situation, search for a fee-only financial advisor in networks like the National Association of Personal Financial Advisors, the Garrett Planning Network (charging hourly fees), the Alliance of Comprehensive Planners (charging an annual retainer and doing tax preparation), and the XY Planning Network (charging a monthly fee and specializing in Gen X and Y clients).

napfa.com

garrettplanningnetwork.com

acplanners.org

❏ In choosing a financial advisor, look for well-respected credentials like the CFP®, ChFC, and CPA/PFS designations.

❏ Check out each advisor's disciplinary records.

brokercheck.finra.org

❏ Continue your due diligence by scheduling interviews with at least three advisors.

❏ If you don't need to search for a financial advisor because you have an advisor you're happy with, schedule a time to review your financial situation and your plan for working together.

**7. Plan for your financial independence.**

❏ Run a retirement calculator to see how much you need to save for your retirement.

https://ffcalcs.com/retirement_estimator

❏ If you can't save enough now, either adjust your retirement goals or look for ways to reduce your expenses or slowly increase your contributions over time. (Your employer's retirement plan may include auto-escalation, a feature that makes this happen automatically.)

❏ Max out your tax-advantaged accounts (like your HSA, your employer's retirement plan, or your IRA) before saving in a taxable account.

❏ If you have partnered with a financial planner, that person should be able to run spreadsheets for you in order to forecast your current and future retirement situation based on your current contributions and income. If your planner either cannot make this forecast or has to find a third party to do it, this may be a red flag that you're working with a bogus financial advisor.

**8. Plan for education expenses.**

❏ Calculate how much financial aid your child may be eligible for.

finaid.org/calculators/finaidestimate.phtml

❏ If you're on track for retirement, calculate how much to save
for your education funding goals.

> apps.finra.org/calcs/1/collegesavings

❏ Contribute your education savings to a 529 plan or a Coverdell
education savings account.

> savingforcollege.com

## 9. Optimize your investments.

❏ To determine how your investments should be diversified
based on your time frame and comfort with risk, fill out a risk
tolerance questionnaire, such as the Risk Tolerance Questionnaire and Asset Allocation Worksheet available through
Financial Finesse.

> secure.financialfinesse.com/go/2997

❏ Look for low-cost investment options such as index funds.

> morningstar.com
>
> vanguard.com
>
> fidelity.com

❏ Consider keeping things simple with a one-stop solution like
a balanced fund, a target date fund for retirement, or an age-
based portfolio for education.

❏ Decide whether you have the expertise to manage your
investments in a tax-efficient manner or whether you need to
hire a financial advisor to help you.

❏ Is your financial advisor either skittish about advising you on
the preceding items or intent on one specific investment or
strategy? These may be signs that your advisor is more inter-
ested in his or her own gains than yours. Consider whether it's
time to find a new advisor.

❏ If you choose to pick your own investments, determine
whether your account has an automatic rebalancing feature
or whether you need to schedule a time to rebalance it yourself
at least once a year.

## 10. Make sure you and your family are protected.

❏ Check your health, property and casualty, life, and disability insurance policies to make sure you have adequate coverage. See if you or your financial advisor can get better deals through your employer or on the private marketplace.

❑ Consider purchasing long-term care insurance if you have between $200,000 and $2 million in assets and are in your fifties to early sixties.

❑ Make sure that your beneficiary designations, your will, your durable power of attorney, and your advance health care directive are up-to-date.

❑ If you have a living trust, check that it's up-to-date and fully funded. If you don't have a trust, see what you can do to avoid probate in your state.

> nolo.com/legal-encyclopedia/avoiding-probate-in-your -state-31015.html

❑ If you need to draft or update any legal documents, see if you can get free or low-cost estate planning assistance through your employer.

❑ *Important!* Let your loved ones know how to access critical documents and other information if something were to happen to you.

Congratulations! It's time to celebrate! You've just taken the first basic steps to becoming financially independent and secure. Considering what a difference small savings and key decisions can make, you have just set up a plan that is likely to result in hundreds of thousands of dollars or more over time. And you've set the wheels in motion for a better, more fulfilling life for yourself and your loved ones.

But like any process, it doesn't end here. Go to financialfinesse.com /financialindependenceday to continue the journey and become part of a community of people dedicated to becoming financially secure and inspiring others to do so as well.

Happy Financial Independence Day!

# Acknowledgments

**Thank you to** Rick Wolff, and the whole team at Houghton Mifflin Harcourt, for the much-needed edits, support, guidance, and patience throughout the process of writing this book. Rick, thank you for taking a chance on me and bringing me the book I wanted to write before I knew I wanted to write it.

To Michele Matrisciani, who helped me find my voice and keep it real. Many of the best parts of this book were written, edited, or inspired by you.

To Adam Chromy for your vision, guidance, and Jedi Mind tricks. Even when I was determined to make the wrong decisions about navigating the world of publishing, you saved me from myself.

To Joe Cullinane for being the best mentor anyone could ever ask for.

To my team—Kelsey Anderson, who kept me sane, managed the chaos, and edited this with incredible skill and grace under pressure; Erik Carter for all the research, feedback, and insights, especially on investing and tax planning; Danielle Encinas, Tania Brown, Daphne Winston, Greg Ward, and the Financial Finesse Think Tank—you earned a kidney. And now it's in writing!

To Dan Starobin, Bruce Young, Linda Robertson, Shannon Carlson, and Oleg Baranovsky for your respective parts in running this great company and making it better and stronger than I ever could. And to Beth Consalvi and Nelson and Gina Caraballo—you are family now whether you like it or not!

Lastly to the loves of my life, Joe and Jay Casale, thank you for your unconditional love and support. Nothing matters without you.

# Index